THE AMERICAN CREDO

BY H. L. MENCKEN AND GEORGE JEAN NATHAN

HELIOGABALUS: A BUFFOONERY

BY H. L. MENCKEN

THE PHILOSOPHY OF FRIEDRICH NIETZSCHE

A BOOK OF BURLESQUES

IN DEFENSE OF WOMEN

A BOOK OF PREFACES

PREJUDICES: FIRST SERIES

"   SECOND "

THE AMERICAN LANGUAGE

BY GEORGE JEAN NATHAN

ANOTHER BOOK ON THE THEATRE

MR. GEORGE JEAN NATHAN PRESENTS

A BOOK WITHOUT A TITLE

THE POPULAR THEATRE

COMEDIANS ALL

THE THEATRE, THE DRAMA, THE GIRLS,

THE CRITIC AND THE DRAMA

THE AMERICAN CREDO

A Contribution Toward the Interpretation
of the National Mind

Revised and Enlarged Edition

BY

GEORGE JEAN NATHAN
and H. L. MENCKEN

NEW YORK
ALFRED · A · KNOPF
1921

PREFACES

PREFACE TO THE REVISED AND ENLARGED EDITION

This edition embodies a number of changes, some of omission and some of addition. The imperfections of the original work were obvious to us when we sent it forth, and we are very grateful to those scholars at home and abroad who have contributed so generously to its improvement. In particular, we owe a large debt to Mr. Aubrey Donaldson, M. A., Reader in Comparative Mythology at Oxford, and to Prof. Dr. Gustav Simmelmeyer, of the University of Zürich. Dr. Simmelmeyer printed a long and very learned review of the work in the *Schweizerisches Archiv für Volkskunde*, and it was instrumental in establishing pleasant contacts with distinguished folk-lorists in various European countries, notably Dr. Arnold Letkow of Berlin, Prof. Ledoux of the Sorbonne, Dr. Enrico Forelli of Turin, and Prof. Mendoza of Salamanca, editor of the well-known *Biblioteca de las tradiciones españolas*. Prof. Mendoza was good enough to say that the book showed a revolu-

[3]

tionary point of departure in the study of the origin and growth of myths, and to propose that a
series of volumes upon the same plan be undertaken by European savants, each dealing with his
own country. This proposal has met with a response in Sweden, where Dr. Gothemann, lecturer
upon Oral Literatures at Upsala, has undertaken
a Swedish work of like character, and in Germany,
where various articles dealing with German popular beliefs in the same manner have been printed
in the *Beiträge zur Volks- und Völkerkunde*,
chiefly from the able pens of Prof. Kuno Goertz
and Baron Hereward von Albrechtsein. We are
also informed that a Bulgarian ethnologist has
undertaken a collection, and that a monograph
upon Italian folk-history, by Prof. Forelli, is soon
to be published in the *Archivio per lo studio delle
tradizioni populari* of Palermo.

From observers nearer home we have received
a great deal of aid. In fact, it would fill several
pages merely to print the names of those who have
kindly favoured us with additions to our collection,
and with criticisms of the matter already printed.
In the case of the latter we have found it necessary
to make few changes. The first edition was in-

complete, but we believe that, in the main, it was accurate. In conclusion we have to offer our thanks to the authorities of the Smithsonian Institution and to various members of the American Folk-Lore Society and the American Anthropological Association for important suggestions. Some of the material, of course, is in a state of flux; as the years pass popular beliefs change. We hope, at intervals, to revise the book, and we shall be grateful for contributions and criticisms.

G.J.N.
H.L.M.

New York, January 1, 1922.

PREFACE TO THE FIRST EDITION

I

The superficial, no doubt, will mistake this little book for a somewhat laborious attempt at jocosity. Because, incidentally to its main purpose, it unveils occasional ideas of so inordinate an erroneousness that they verge upon the ludicrous, it will be set down a piece of spoofing, and perhaps denounced as in bad taste. But all the while that main purpose will remain clear enough to the judicious. It is, in brief, the purpose of clarifying the current exchange of rhetorical gas-bombs upon the subject of American ideals and the American character, so copious, so cocksure and withal so ill-informed and inconclusive, by putting into plain propositions some of the notions that lie at the heart of those ideals and enter into the very substance of that character. "For as he thinketh in his heart," said Solomon, "so *is* he." It is a saying, obviously, that one may easily fill with fan-

[7]

tastic meanings, as the prevailing gabble of the mental healers, New Thoughters, efficiency engineers, professors of scientific salesmanship and other such mountebanks demonstrates, but nevertheless it is one grounded, at bottom, upon an indubitable fact. Deep down in every man there is a body of congenital attitudes, a corpus of ineradicable doctrines and ways of thinking, that determines his reactions to his ideational environment as surely as his physical activity is determined by the length of his *tibiæ* and the capacity of his lungs. These primary attitudes, in fact, constitute the essential man. It is by recognition of them that one arrives at an accurate understanding of his place and function as a member of human society; it is by a shrewd reckoning and balancing of them, one against another, that one forecasts his probable behaviour in the face of unaccustomed stimuli.

All the arts and sciences that have to do with the management of men in the mass are founded upon a proficient practice of that sort of reckoning. The practical politician, as every connoisseur of ochlocracy knows, is not a man who seeks to inoculate the innumerable caravan of voters with new ideas; he is a man who seeks to search out and prick into energy the basic ideas that are already in them, and to turn the resultant effervescence of emotion to his own uses. And so with the religious teacher, the social and economic reformer, and every other variety of popular educator, down to and including the humblest press-agent of a fifth assistant Secretary of State, moving-picture actor, or Y. M. C. A. boob-squeezing committee. Such adept professors of conviction and enthusiasm, in the true sense, never actually teach anything new; all they do is to give new forms to beliefs already in being, to arrange the bits of glass, onyx, horn, ivory, porphyry and corundum in the mental kaleidoscope of the populace into novel permutations. To change the figure, they may give the medulla oblongata, the cerebral organ of the great masses of simple men, a powerful diuretic or emetic, but they seldom, if ever, add anything to its primary supply of fats, proteids and carbohydrates.

One speaks of the great masses of simple men, and it is of them, of course, that the ensuing treatise chiefly has to say. The higher and more delicately organized tribes and sects of men are susceptible to no such ready anatomizing, for the body of be-

[9]

liefs upon which their ratiocination grounds itself is not fixed but changing, and not artless and
crystal-clear but excessively complex and obscure.
It is, indeed, the chief mark of a man emerged
from the general that he has lost most of his original certainties, and is full of a scepticism which
plays like a spray of acid upon all the ideas
that come within his purview, including especially
his own. One does not become surer as one ad-
vances in knowledge, but less sure. No article of
faith is proof against the disintegrating effects of
increasing information; one might almost describe
the acquirement of knowledge as a process of dis-
illusion. But among the humbler ranks of men
who make up the great bulk of every civilized people the increase of information is so slow and so
arduous that this effect is scarcely to be discerned.
If, in the course of long years, they gradually lose
their old faiths, it is only to fill the gaps with new
faiths that restate the old ones in new terms. Nothing, in fact, could be more commonplace than the
observation that the crazes which periodically ravage the proletariat today are, in the main, no more
than distorted echoes of delusions cherished cen-
turies ago. The fundamental religious ideas of the

lower orders of Christendom have not changed materially in two thousand years, and they were old when they were first borrowed from the heathen of northern Africa and Asia Minor. The Iowa Methodist of today, imagining him competent to understand them at all, would be able to accept the tenets of Augustine without changing more than a few accents and punctuation marks. Every Sunday his raucous ecclesiastics batter his ears with diluted and debased filches from *De Civitate Dei,* and almost every article of his practical ethics may be found clearly stated in the eminent bishop's Ninety-third Epistle. And so in politics. The Bolsheviki of the present not only poll-parrot the balderdash of the French demagogues of 1789; they also mouth what was gospel to every *bête blonde* in the Teutonic forest of the fifth century. Truth shifts and changes like a cataract of diamonds; its aspect is never precisely the same at two successive instants. But error flows down the channel of history like some great stream of lava or infinitely lethargic glacier. It is the one relatively fixed thing in a world of chaos. It is, perhaps, the one thing that gives human society the small stability that it needs, amid all the oscillation of a gelatinous cosmos, to

[11]

save it from the wreck that ever menaces. Without their dreams men would have fallen upon and devoured one another long ago—and yet every dream is an illusion, and every illusion is a lie.

Nevertheless, this immutability of popular ideas is not quite perfect. The main current, no doubt, goes on unbrokenly, but there are many eddies along the edges and many small tempests on the surface. Thus the aspect changes, if not the substance. What men believe in one century is apparently abandoned in some other century, and perhaps supplanted by something quite to the contrary. Or, at all events, to the contrary in appearance. Off goes the head of the king, and tyranny gives way to freedom. The change seems abysmal. Then, bit by bit, the face of freedom hardens, and by and by it is the old face of tyranny. Then another cycle, and another. But under the play of all these opposites there is something fundamental and permanent—the basic delusion that men may be governed and yet be free. It is only on the surface that there are transformations— and these we must study and make the most of, for of what is underneath men are mainly unconscious. The thing that colours the upper levels is largely the instinctive functioning of race and nationality, the ineradicable rivalry of tribe and tribe, the primary struggle for existence. At bottom, no doubt, the plain men of the whole world are almost indistinguishably alike; a learned anthropologist, Prof. Dr. Boas, has written a book to prove it. But, collected into herds, they gather delusions that are special to herds. Beside the underlying mass thinking there is a superimposed group thinking— a sort of unintelligent class consciousness. This we may prod into. This, in the case of the *Homo americanus,* is what is prodded into in the present work. We perform, it seems to us, a useful pioneering. Incomplete though our data may be, it is at least grounded upon a resolute avoidance of *a priori* methods, an absolutely open-minded effort to get at the facts. We pounce upon them as they bob up, convinced that even the most inconsiderable of them may have its profound significance— that the essential may be hidden in the trivial. All we aim at is a first marshalling of materials, an initial running of lines. We are not architects, but furnishers of bricks, nails and laths. But it is our hope that what we thus rake up and pile into a rough heap may yet serve the purposes of

[13]

an organizer, and so help toward the establishment of the dim and vacillating truth, and rid the scene of, at all events, the worst and most obvious of its present accumulation of errors.

II

In the case of the American of the multitude that accumulation of errors is of astounding bulk and consequence. His ideas are not only grossly misapprehended by all foreigners; they are often misapprehended by his own countrymen of superior education, and even by himself.

This last, at first blush, may seem a mere effort at paradox, but its literal truth becomes patent on brief inspection. Ask the average American what is the salient passion in his emotional armamentarium—what is the idea that lies at the bottom of all his other ideas—and it is very probable that, nine times out of ten, he will nominate his hot and unquenchable rage for liberty. He regards himself, indeed, as the chief exponent of liberty in the whole world, and all its other advocates as no more than his followers, half timorous and half envious. To question his ardour is to insult him as grievously as if one questioned the honour of

[14]

the republic or the chastity of his wife. And yet it must be plain to any dispassionate observer that this ardour, in the course of a century and a half, has lost a large part of its old burning reality and descended to the estate of a mere phosphorescent superstition. The American of today, in fact, probably enjoys less personal liberty than any other man of Christendom, and even his political liberty is fast succumbing to the new dogma that certain theories of government are virtuous and lawful and others abhorrent and felonious. Laws limiting the radius of his free activity multiply year by year: it is now practically impossible for him to exhibit anything describable as genuine individuality, either in action or in thought, without running afoul of some harsh and unintelligible penalty. It would surprise no impartial observer if the motto, *In God we trust,* were one day expunged from the coins of the republic by the Junkers at Washington, and the far more appropriate word, *Verboten,* substituted. Nor would it astound any save the most romantic if, at the same time, the goddess of liberty were taken off the silver dollars to make room for a bas relief of a policeman in a spiked helmet.

Moreover, this gradual (and, of late, rapidly progressive) decay of freedom goes almost without challenge; the American has grown so accustomed to the denial of his constitutional rights and to the minute regulation of his conduct by swarms of spies, letter-openers, informers and *agents provocateurs* that he no longer makes any serious protest. It is surely a significant fact that, in the face of the late almost incredible proceedings under the so-called Espionage Act and other such laws, the only objections heard of came either from the persons directly affected—nine-tenths of them Socialists, pacifists, or citizens accused of German sympathies, and hence without any rights whatever in American law and equity—or from a small group of professional libertarians, chiefly naturalized aliens. The American people, as a people, acquiesced docilely in all these tyrannies, both during the war and after the war, just as they acquiesced in the invasion of their common rights by the Prohibition Amendment. Worse, they not only acquiesced docilely; they approved actively; they were quite as hotly against the few protestants as they were against the original victims, and gave their hearty approbation to every proposal that

[16]

the former be punished too. The really startling phenomenon of the war, indeed, was not the grotesque abolition of liberty in the name of liberty, but the failure of that usurpation to arouse anything approaching public indignation. It is impossible to imagine the men of Jackson's army or even of Grant's army submitting to any such absolutism without a furious struggle, but in these latter days it is viewed with the utmost complacency. The descendants of the Americans who punished John Adams so melodramatically for the Alien and Seditions Acts of 1789 failed to raise a voice against the far more drastic legislation of 1917. What is more, they failed to raise a voice against its execution upon the innocent as well as upon the guilty, in gross violation of the most elemental principles of justice and rules of law.

Thus the Americano, put to the test, gave the lie to what is probably his proudest boast, and revealed the chronic human incapacity for accurate self-analysis. But if he thereby misjudged and misjudges himself, he may find some consolation for his error in the lavishness with which even worse misjudgment is heaped upon him by foreigners. To this day, despite the intimate contact

[17]

of five long years of joint war, the French and the
English are ignorant of his true character, and
show it in their every discussion of him, particularly when they discuss him in camera. It is the
secret but general view of the French, we are informed by confidential agents, that he is a fellow
of loose life and not to be trusted with either a
wine-pot, a virgin or a domestic fowl—an absurdly
inaccurate generalization from the aberrations of
soldiers in a far land, cut off from the moral repressions that lie upon them and colour all their acts
at home. It is the view of the English, so we hear
upon equally reliable authority, that he is an earnest but extremely inefficient oaf, incapable of
either the finer technic of war or of its machine-
like discipline—another thumping error, for the
American is actually extraordinarily adept and
ingenious in the very arts that modern war chiefly
makes use of, and there is, since the revolt of the
Prussian, no other such rigidly regimented man
in the world. He has, indeed, reached such a pass
in the latter department that it has become almost
impossible for him to think of himself save as an
obedient member of some vast, powerful and unin-
telligibly despotic organization—a church, a trades-

union, a political party, a tin-pot fraternal order, or what not—, and often he is a member of more than one, and impartially faithful to all. Moreover, as we have seen, he lives under laws which dictate almost every detail of his public and private conduct, and punish every sign of bad discipline with the most appalling rigour; and these laws are enforced by police who supply the chance gaps in them extempore, and exercise that authority in the best manner of prison guards, animal trainers and drill sergeants.

The English and the French, beside these special errors, have a full share in an error that is also embraced by practically every other foreign people. This is the error of assuming, almost as an axiom beyond question, that the Americans are a sordid, money-grubbing people, with no thought above the dollar. You will find it prevailing everywhere on the Continent of Europe. To the German the United States is Dollarica, and the salient American personality, next to the policeman who takes bribes and the snuffling moralist in office, is the Dollarprinzessin. To the Italian the country is a sort of savage wilderness in which everything else, from religion to beauty and from decent re-

[19]

pose to human life, is sacrificed to profit. Italians cross the ocean in much the same spirit that our runaway school-boys used to go off to fight the Indians. Some, lucky, return home in a few years with fortunes and gaudy tales; others, succumbing to the natives, are butchered at their labour and buried beneath the cinders of hideous and God-forsaken mining towns. All carry the thought of escape from beginning to end; every Italian hopes to get away with his takings as soon as possible, to enjoy them on some hillside where life and property are reasonably safe from greed. So with the Russian, the Scandinavian, the Balkan hillman, even the Greek and Armenian. The picture of America that they conjure up is a picture of a titanic and merciless struggle for gold, with the stakes high and the contestants correspondingly ferocious. They see the American as one to whom nothing under the sun has any value save the dollar—not truth, or beauty, or philosophical ease, or the common decencies between man and man.

This view, of course, is full of distortion and misunderstanding, despite the fact that even Americans, by hearing it stated so often, have come to allow it a good deal of soundness. The American's concept of himself, as we have seen, is sometimes anything but accurate; in this case he errs almost as greatly as when he venerates himself as the prince of freemen, with gyveless wrists and flashing eyes. As for the foreigner, what he falls into is the typically Freudian blunder of projecting his own worst weakness into another. The fact is that it is he, and not the native American, who is the incorrigible and unimaginative money-grubber. He comes to the United States in search of money, and in search of money alone, and pursuing that single purpose without deviation he makes the mistake of assuming that the American is at the same business, and in the same fanatical manner. From all the complex and colourful life of the country, save only the one enterprise of money-making, he is shut off almost hermetically, and so he concludes that that one enterprise embraces the whole show. Here the unreliable promptings of his sub-conscious passion are helped out by observations that are more logical. Unfamiliar with the language, excluded from all free social intercourse with the native, and regarded as, if actually human at all, then at least a distinctly inferior member of the species, he is forced into the harshest and most ill-paid labour, and so he inevitably sees the American as a pitiless task-master and ascribes the exploitation he is made a victim of to a fabulous exaggeration of his own avarice.

Moreover, the greater success and higher position of the native seem to bear out this notion. In a struggle that is free for all and to the death, the native grabs all the shiniest stakes. *Ergo,* he must love money even more than the immigrant. This logic we do not defend, but there is —and out of it grows the prevailing foreign view of America and the Americans, for the foreigner who stays at home does not derive his ideas from the glittering, lascivious phrases of Dr. Wilson or from the passionate idealism of such superior Americans as Otto H. Kahn, Adolph S. Ochs, S. Stanwood Menken, Jacob H. Schiff, Marcus Loew, Henry Morgenthau, Abram Elkus, Samuel Goldfish, Louis D. Brandeis, Julius Rosenwald, Paul Warburg, Judge Otto Rosalsky, Adolph Zukor, the Hon. Julius Kahn, Simon Guggenheim, Stephen S. Wise and Barney Baruch, but from the 'hair-raising tales of returned "Americans," *i.e.,* fellow peasants who, having braved the dragons, have come back to the fatherland to enjoy their booty and exhibit their wounds.

[22]

The native, as we say, has been so far influenced by this error that he cherishes it himself, or, more accurately, entertains it with shame. Most of his windy idealism is no more than a reaction against it—an evidence of an effort to confute it and live it down. He is never more sweetly flattered than when some politician eager for votes or some evangelist itching for a good plate tells him that he is actually a soaring altruist, and the only real one in the world. This is the surest way to fetch him; he never fails to swell out his chest when he hears that buncombe. In point of fact, of course, he is no more an altruist than any other healthy mammal. His ideals, one and all, are grounded upon self-interest, or upon the fear that is at the bottom of it; his benevolence always has a string tied to it; he could no more formulate a course of action to his certain disadvantage than an Englishman could, or a Frenchman, or an Italian, or a German. But to say that the advantage he pursues is always, or even usually, a monetary one—to argue that he is avaricious, or even, in these later years, a sharp trader—is to spit directly into the eye of the truth. There is probably, indeed, no country in the world in which mere money is held

[23]

in less esteem than in these United States. Even more than the Russian Bolshevik the American democrat regards wealth with suspicion, and its too eager amassment with a bilious eye. Here alone, west of the Dvina, rich men are *ipso facto* scoundrels and *feræ naturæ*, with no rights that any slanderer is bound to respect. Here alone, the possession of a fortune puts a man automatically upon the defensive, and exposes him to special legislation of a rough and inquisitorial character and to the special animosity of judges, district attorneys and juries. It would be a literal impossibility for an Englishman worth $100,000,000 to avoid public office and public honour; it would be equally impossible for an American worth $100,000,000 to obtain either.

Americans, true enough, enjoy an average of prosperity that is above that witnessed in any other country. Their land, with less labour, yields a greater usufruct than other land; they get more money for their industry; they jingle more coin in their pockets than other peoples. But it is a grievous error to mistake that superior opulence for a sign of money-hunger, for they actually hold money very lightly, and spend a great deal more of it than any other race of men and with far less thought of values. The normal French family, it is often said, could live very comfortably for a week upon what the normal American family wastes in a week. There is, among Americans, not the slightest sign of the unanimous French habit of biting every franc, of calculating the cost of every luxury to five places of decimals, of utilizing every scrap, of sleeping with the bankbook under the pillow. Whatever is showy gets their dollars, whether they need it or not, even whether they can afford it or not. They are, so to speak, constantly on a bust, their eyes alert for chances to get rid of their small change.

Consider, for example, the amazing readiness with which they succumb to the imbecile bait of advertising! An American manufacturer, finding himself with a stock of unsalable goods or encountering otherwise a demand that is less than his production, does not have to look, like his English or German colleague, for foreign dumping grounds. He simply packs his surplus in gaudy packages, sends for an advertising agent, joins an Honest-Advertising club, fills the newspapers and magazines with lying advertisements, and sits down in

[25]

peace while his countrymen fight their way to his counters. That they will come is almost absolutely sure; no matter how valueless the goods, they will leap to the advertisements; their one desire seems to be to get rid of their money. As a consequence of this almost pathological eagerness, the advertising bill of the American people is greater than that of all other peoples taken together. There is scarcely an article within the range of their desires that does not carry a heavy load of advertising; they actually pay out millions every year to be sold such commonplace necessities as sugar, towels, collars, lead-pencils and corn-meal. The business of thus bamboozling them and picking their pockets enlists thousands and thousands of artists, writers, printers, sign-painters and other such parasites. Their towns are bedaubed with chromatic eye-sores and made hideous with flashing lights; their countryside is polluted; their newspapers and magazines become mere advertising sheets; idiotic slogans and apothegms are invented to enchant them; in some cities they are actually taxed to advertise the local makers of wooden nutmegs. Multitudes of swindlers are naturally induced to adopt advertising as a trade, and some of

[26]

them make great fortunes at it. Like all other men who live by their wits, they regard themeslves as superior fellows, and every year they hold great conventions, bore each other with learned papers upon the psychology of their victims, speak of one another as men of genius, have themselves photographed by the photographers of newspapers eager to curry favour with them, denounce the government for not spending the public funds for advertising, and summon United States Senators, eminent chautauquans and distinguished vaudeville stars to entertain them. For all this the plain people pay the bill, and never a protest comes out of them.

As a matter of fact, the only genuinely thrifty folks among us, in the sense that a Frenchman, a Scot or an Italian is thrifty, are the immigrants of the most recent invasions. That is why they oust the native wherever the two come into contact— say in New England and in the Middle West. They acquire, bit by bit, the best lands, the best stock, the best barns, not because they have the secret of *making* more money, but because they have the resolution to *spend* less. As soon as they become thoroughly Americanized they begin to show the national prodigality. The old

[27]

folks wear home-made clothes and stick to the farm; the native-born children order their garments from mail-order tailors and expose themselves in the chautauquas and at the great orgies of Calvinism and Wesleyanism. The old folks put every dollar they can wring from a reluctant environment into real property or the banks; the young folks put their inheritance into phonographs, Fords, boiled shirts, yellow shoes, cuckoo clocks, lithographs of the current mountebanks, oil stock, automatic pianos and the works of Harold Bell Wright, Gerald Stanley Lee and O. Henry.

III

But what, then, is the character that actually marks the American—that is, in chief? If he is not the exalted monopolist of liberty that he thinks he is nor the noble altruist and idealist he slaps upon the chest when he is full of rhetoric, nor the degraded dollar-chaser of European legend, then what is he? We offer an answer in all humility, for the problem is complex and there is but little illumination of it in the literature; nevertheless, we offer it in the firm conviction, born of twenty years' incessant meditation, that it is substantially correct.

It is, in brief, this: that the thing which sets off the American from all other men, and gives a peculiar colour not only to the pattern of his daily life but also to the play of his inner ideas, is what, for want of a more exact term, may be called social aspiration. That is to say, his dominant passion is a passion to lift himself by at least a step or two in the society that he is a part of—a passion to improve his position, to break down some shadowy barrier of caste, to achieve the countenance of what, for all his talk of equality, he recognizes and accepts as his betters. The American is a pusher. His eyes are ever fixed upon some round of the ladder that is just beyond his reach, and all his secret ambitions, all his extraordinary energies, group themselves about the yearning to grasp it. Here we have an explanation of the curious restlessness that educated foreigners, as opposed to mere immigrants, always make a note of in the country; it is half aspiration and half impatience, with overtones of dread and timorousness. The American is violently eager to get on, and thoroughly convinced that his merits entitle him to try and to succeed, but by the same token he is sickeningly fearful of slipping back, and out of

[29]

the second fact, as we shall see, spring some of his most characteristic traits. .He is a man vexed, at one and the same time, by delusions of grandeur and an inferiority complex; he is both egotistical and subservient, assertive and politic, blatant and shy. Most of the errors about him are made by seeing one side of him and being blind to the other.

Such a thing as a secure position is practically unknown among us. There is no American who cannot hope to lift himself another notch or two, if he is good; there is absolutely no hard and fast impediment to his progress. But neither is there any American who doesn't have to keep on fighting for whatever position he has; no wall of caste is there to protect him if he slips. One observes every day the movement of individuals, families, whole groups, in both directions. All of our cities are full of brummagem aristocrats—aristocrats, at all events, in the view of their neighbours—whose grandfathers, or even fathers, were day labourers; and working for them, supported by them, heavily patronized by them, are clerks whose grandfathers were lords of the soil. The older societies of Europe, as every one knows, protect their caste lines a great deal more resolutely. It is as impossible for a wealthy pork packer or company promoter to enter the *noblesse* of Austria, even today, as it would be for him to enter the boudoir of a queen; he is barred out absolutely and even his grand-children are under the ban. And in precisely the same way it is as impossible for a count of the old Holy Roman Empire to lose caste as it would be for the Dalai Lama; he may sink to unutterable depths within his order, but he cannot get himself out of it, nor can he lose the peculiar advantages that go with membership; he is still a *Graf*, and, as such, above the herd. Once, in a Madrid café, the two of us encountered a Spanish marquis who wore celluloid cuffs, suffered from pediculosis and had been drunk for sixteen years. Yet he remained a marquis in good standing, and all lesser Spaniards, including Socialists, envied him and deferred to him; none would have dreamed of slapping him on the back. Knowing that he was quite as safe within his ancient order as a dog among the *canidæ*, he gave no thought to appearances. But in the same way he knew that he had reached his limit—that no conceivable effort could lift him higher. He was a grandee of Spain and that was all; above glimmered royalty and the

[31]

hierarchy of the saints, and both royalty and the hierarchy of the saints were as much beyond him as grandeeism was beyond the polite and well-educated head-waiter who laved him with ice-water when he had *mania-a-potu.*

No American is ever so securely lodged. There is always something just ahead of him, beckoning him and tantalizing him, and there is always something just behind him, menacing him and causing him to sweat. Even when he attains to what may seem to be security, that security is very fragile. The English soap-boiler, brewer, shyster attorney or stock-jobber, once he has got into the House of Lords, is reasonably safe, and his children after him; the possession of a peerage connotes a definite rank, and it is as permanent as anything can be in this world. But in America there is no such harbour; the ship is eternally at sea. Money vanishes, official dignity is forgotten, caste lines are as full of gaps as an ill-kept hedge. The grandfather of the Vanderbilts was a bounder; the last of the Washingtons is a petty employé in the Library of Congress.

It is this constant possibility of rising, this constant risk of falling, that gives a barbaric pic-

[32]

turesqueness to the panorama of what is called fashionable society in America. The chief character of that society is to be found in its shameless self-assertion, its almost obscene display of its importance and of the shadowy privileges and acceptances on which that importance is based. It is assertive for the simple reason that, immediately it ceased to be assertive, it would cease to exist. Structurally, it is composed in every town of a nucleus of those who have laboriously arrived and a chaotic mass of those who are straining every effort to get on. The effort must be made against great odds. Those who have arrived are eager to keep down the competition of newcomers; on their exclusiveness, as the phrase is, rests the whole of their social advantage. Thus the candidate from below, before horning in at last, must put up with an infinity of rebuff and humiliation; he must sacrifice his self-respect today in order to gain the hope of destroying the self-respect of other aspirants tomorrow. The result is that the whole edifice is based upon fears and abasements, and that every device which promises to protect the individual against them is seized upon eagerly. Fashionable society in America therefore has no room

[33]

for intelligence; within its fold an original idea is
dangerous; it carries regimentation, in dress, in social customs and in political and even religious
doctrines, to the last degree. In the American
cities the fashionable man or woman must not
only maintain the decorum seen among civilized
folks everywhere; he or she must also be inter-
ested in precisely the right sports, theatrical shows
and opera singers, show the right political creduli-
ties and indignations, and have some sort of con-
nection with the right church. Nearly always, because of the apeing of English custom that pre-
vails everywhere in America, it must be the so-
called Protestant Episcopal Church, a sort of out-
house of the Church of England, with ecclesiastics
who imitate the English sacerdotal manner much
as small boys imitate the manner of eminent baseball players. Every fashionable Protestant Episcopal congregation in the land is full of ex-Bap-
tists and ex-Methodists who have shed Calvinism,
total immersion and the hallelujah hymns on their
way up the ladder. The same impulse leads the
Jews, whenever the possibility of invading the cita-
del of the Christians begins to bemuse them (as
happened during the late war, for example, when

[34]

patriotism temporarily adjourned the usual taboos), to embrace Christian Science—as a sort of half-way station, so to speak, more medical than Christian, and hence secure against ordinary derisions. And it is an impulse but little different which lies at the bottom of the much-discussed title-hunt.

A title, however paltry, is of genuine social value, more especially in America; it represents a status that cannot be changed overnight by the rise of rivals, or by personal dereliction, or by mere accident. It is a policy of insurance against dangers that are not to be countered as effectively in any other manner. Miss G——, the daughter of an enormously wealthy scoundrel, may be accepted everywhere, but all the while she is insecure. Her father may lose his fortune tomorrow, or be jailed by newspaper outcry, or marry a prostitute and so commit social suicide himself and murder his daughter, or she herself may fall a victim to some rival's superior machinations, or stoop to fornication of some forbidden variety, or otherwise get herself under the ban. But once she is a duchess, she is safe. No catastrophe short of divorce can take away her coronet, and even divorce will leave the purple marks of it upon her brow. Most

[35]

valuable boon of all, she is now free to be herself, —a rare, rare experience for an American. She may, if she likes, go about in a Mother Hubbard, or join the Seventh Day Adventists, or declare for the Bolsheviki, or wash her own lingerie, or have her hair bobbed, and still she will remain a duchess, and, as a duchess, irremovably superior to the gaping herd of her political equals.

This social aspiration, of course, is most vividly violent and idiotic on its higher and more gaudy levels, but it is scarcely less earnest below. Every American, however obscure, has formulated within his secret recesses some concept of advancement, however meagre; if he doesn't aspire to be what is called fashionable, then he at least aspires to lift himself in some less gorgeous way. There is not a social organization in this land of innumerable associations that hasn't its waiting list of candidates who are eager to get in, but have not yet demonstrated their fitness for the honour. One can scarcely go low enough to find that pressure absent. Even the tin-pot fraternal orders, which are constantly cadging for members and seem to accept any one not a downright felon, are exclusive in their fantastic way, and no doubt there are hundreds of thousands of proud American freemen, the heirs of Washington and Jefferson, their liberty safeguarded by a million guns, who pine in secret because they are ineligible to membership in the Masons, the Odd Fellows or even the Knights of Pythias. On the distaff side, the thing is too obvious to need exposition. The patriotic societies among women are all machines for the resuscitation of lost superiorities. The plutocracy has shouldered out the old gentry from actual social leadership—that gentry, indeed, presents a prodigious clinical picture of the insecurity of social rank in America—but there remains at least the possibility of insisting upon a dignity which plutocrats cannot boast and may not even buy. Thus the county judge's wife in Smithville or the Methodist pastor's daughter in Jonestown consoles herself for the lack of an opera box with the thought (constantly asserted by badge and resolution) that she had a nobler grandfather, or, at all events, a decenter one, than the Astors, the Vanderbilts and the Goulds.

[37]

IV

It seems to us that the genuine characters of the normal American, the characters which set him off most saliently from the men of other nations, are the fruits of all this risk of and capacity for change in status that we have described, and of the dreads and hesitations that go therewith. The American is marked, in fact, by precisely the habits of mind and act that one would look for in a man insatiably ambitious and yet incurably fearful, to wit, the habits, on the one hand, of unpleasant assertiveness, of somewhat boisterous braggardism, of incessant pushing, and, on the other hand, of conformity, caution and subservience. He is forever talking of his rights as if he stood ready to defend them with his last drop of blood, and forever yielding them up at the first demand. Under both the pretension and the fact is the common motive of fear—in brief, the common motive of the insecure and uncertain man, the *average* man, at all times and everywhere, but especially the motive of the average man in a social system so crude and unstable as ours.

"More than any other people," said Wendell

[38]

Phillips one blue day, "we Americans are afraid of one another." The saying seems harsh. It goes counter to the national delusion of uncompromising courage and limitless truculence. It wars upon the national vanity. But all the same there is truth in it. Here, more than anywhere else on earth, the status of an individual is determined by the general consent of the general body of his fellows; here, as we have seen, there are no artificial barriers to protect him against their disapproval, or even against their envy. And here, more than anywhere else, the general consent of that general body of men is coloured by the ideas and prejudices of the inferior majority; here, there is the nearest approach to genuine democracy, the most direct and accurate response to mob emotions. Facing that infinitely powerful but inevitably ignorant and cruel corpus of opinion, the individual must needs adopt caution and fall into timorousness. The desire within him may be bold and forthright, but its satisfaction demands discretion, prudence, a politic and ingratiating habit. The walls are not to be stormed; they must be wooed to a sort of Jerichoan fall. Success thus takes the form of a series of waves of protective colouration; failure is a succession of unmaskings. The aspirant must first learn to imitate exactly the aspect and behaviour of the group he seeks to penetrate. There follows notice. There follows toleration. There follows acceptance.

Thus the hog-murderer's wife picks her way into the society of Chicago, the proud aristocracy of the abbatoir. And thus, no less, the former whiskey drummer insinuates himself into the Elks, and the rising retailer wins the *imprimatur* of wholesalers, and the rich peasant becomes a planter and the father of doctors of philosophy, and the servant girl enters the movies and acquires the status of a princess of the blood, and the petty attorney becomes a legislator and statesman, and Schmidt turns into Smith, and the newspaper reporter becomes a *littérateur* on the staff of the *Saturday Evening Post*, and all of us Yankees creep up, up, up. The business is never to be accomplished by headlong assault. It must be done circumspectly, insidiously, a bit apologetically, *pianissimo;* there must be no flaunting of unusual ideas, no bold prancing of an unaccustomed personality. Above all, it must be done without exciting fear, lest the portcullis fall and the whole enterprise go to pot.

Above all, the manner of a Jenkins must be got into it.

That manner, of course, is not incompatible with a certain superficial boldness, nor even with an appearance of truculence. But what lies beneath the boldness is not really an independent spirit, but merely a talent for crying with the pack. When the American is most dashingly assertive it is a sure sign that he feels the pack behind him, and hears its comforting baying, and is well aware that his doctrine is approved. He is not a joiner for nothing. He joins something, whether it be a political party, a church, a fraternal order or one of the idiotic movements that incessantly ravage the land, because joining gives him a feeling of security, because it makes him a part of something larger and safer than he is himself, because it gives him a chance to work off steam without running any risk. The whole thinking of the country thus runs down the channel of mob emotion; there is no actual conflict of ideas, but only a succession of crazes. It is inconvenient to stand aloof from these crazes, and it is dangerous to oppose them. In no other country in the world is there so ferocious a short way with dissenters; in none other is it socially so costly to heed the inner voice and to be one's own man.

Thus encircled by taboos, the American shows an extraordinary timorousness in all his dealings with fundamentals, and the fact that many of these taboos are self-imposed only adds to their rigour. What every observant foreigner first notices, canvassing the intellectual life of the land, is the shy and gingery manner in which all the larger problems of existence are dealt with. We have, for example, positive laws which make it practically impossible to discuss the sex question with anything approaching honesty. The literature of the subject is enormous, and the general notion of its importance is thereby made manifest, but all save a very small part of that literature is produced by quacks and addressed to an audience that is afraid to hear the truth. So in politics. Almost alone among the civilized nations of the world, the United States pursues critics of the dominant political theory with mediaeval ferocity, condemning them to interminable periods in prison, proceeding against them by clamour and perjury, treating them worse than common blacklegs, and at times conniving at their actual murder by the police. And so, above all, in religion. This is the only country of Christendom in which there is no anti-clerical party, and hence no constant and effective criticism of clerical pretension and corruption. The result is that all of the churches reach out for tyranny among us, and that most of them that show any numerical strength already exercise it. In half a dozen of our largest cities the Catholic Church is actually a good deal more powerful than it is in Spain, or even in Austria. Its acts are wholly above public discussion; it makes and breaks public officials; it holds the newspapers in terror; it influences the police and the courts; it is strong enough to destroy and silence any man who objects to its polity. But this is not all. The Catholic Church, at worst, is an organization largely devoted to perfectly legitimate and even laudable purposes, and it is controlled by a class of men who are largely above popular passion, and intelligent enough to see beyond the immediate advantage. More important still, its international character gives it a detached and superior point of view, and so makes it stand aloof from some of the common weaknesses of the native mob. This is constantly revealed by its opposition to Prohibition, vice-crusading and other such crazes of the disinherited and unhappy. The rank and file of its members are ignorant and emotional and are thus almost ideal cannon-fodder for the bogus reformers who operate upon the proletariat, but they are held back by their clergy, to whose superior interest in genuine religion is added a centuries-old heritage of worldly wisdom. Thus the Church of Rome, in America at least, is a civilizing agency, and we may well overlook its cynical alliance with political corruption in view of its steady enmity to that greater corruption which destroys the very elements of liberty, peace and human dignity. It may be a bit too intelligently selfish and harshly realistic, but it is assuredly not swinish.

This adjective, however, fits the opposition as snugly as a coat of varnish—and by the opposition we mean the group of Protestant churches commonly called evangelical, to wit, the Methodist, the Baptist, the Presbyterian and their attendant imitators and inferiors. It is out of this group that the dominating religious attitude of the American people arises, and, in particular, it is from this group that we get our doctrine that religious activity is not to be challenged, however flagrantly it may

[44]

stand in opposition to common honesty and common sense. Under cover of that artificial toleration—the product, not of a genuine liberalism, but simply of a mob distrust of dissent—there goes on a tyranny that it would be difficult to match in modern history. Save in a few large cities, every American community lies under a sacerdotal despotism whose devices are disingenuous and dishonourable, and whose power was magnificently displayed in the campaign for Prohibition—a despotism exercised by a body of ignorant, superstitious, self-seeking and thoroughly dishonest men. One may, without prejudice, reasonably defend the Catholic clergy. They are men who, at worst, pursue an intelligible ideal and dignify it with a real sacrifice. But in the presence of the Methodist clergy it is difficult to avoid giving way to the weakness of indignation. What one observes is a horde of uneducated and inflammatory dunderheads, eager for power, intolerant of opposition and full of a childish vanity—a mob of holy clerks but little raised, in intelligence and dignity, above the forlorn half-wits whose souls they chronically rack. In the whole United States there is scarcely one among them who stands forth as a man of sense and

[45]

information. Illiterate in all save the elementals, untouched by the larger currents of thought, drunk with their power over dolts, crazed by their immunity to challenge by their betters, they carry over into the professional class of the country the spirit of the most stupid peasantry, and degrade religion to the estate of an idiotic phobia. There is not a village in America in which some such preposterous jackass is not in eruption. Worse, he is commonly the leader of its opinion—its pattern in reason, morals and good taste. Yet worse, he is ruler as well as pattern. Wrapped in his sacerdotal cloak, he stands above any effective criticism. To question his imbecile ideas is to stand in contumacy of the revelation of God.

A number of years ago, while engaged in journalism in a large American city, one of us violated all journalistic precedents by printing an article denouncing the local evangelical clergy as, with few exceptions, a pack of scoundrels, and offered in proof their brisk and constant trade in contraband marriages, especially the marriages of girls under the age of consent. He showed that the offer of a two dollar fee was sufficient to induce the majority of these ambassadors of Christ to marry

[46]

a girl of fourteen or fifteen to a boy a few years older. There followed a great outcry from the accused, with the usual demands that the offending paper print a retraction and discharge the guilty writer from its staff. He thereupon engaged a clipping bureau to furnish him with clippings from the newspapers of the whole country, showing the common activities of the evangelical clergy elsewhere. The result was that he received and reprinted an amazing mass of putrid scandal, greatly to the joy of that moral community. It appeared that these eminent Christian leaders were steadily engaged, North, East, South and West, in doings that would have disgraced so many ward heelers or oyster-shuckers—shady financial transactions, gross sexual irregularities, all sorts of minor crimes. The publication of this evidence from day to day gave the chronicler the advantage of the offensive, and so got him out of a tight place. In the end, as if tickled by his assault, the hierarchy of heaven came to his aid. That is to say, the Lord God Jehovah arranged it that one of the leading Methodist clergymen of the city—in fact, the chronicler's chief opponent—should be taken in an unmentionable sexual perversion at the head-

[47]

quarters of the Young Men's Christian Association, and so be forced to leave town between days. This catastrophe, as we say, the chronicler ascribes to divine intervention. It was entirely unexpected; he knew that the fellow was a liar and a rogue, but he had never suspected that he was also a hog. The episode demoralized the defence to such an extent that it was impossible, in decency, to go on with the war. The chronicler was at once, in fact, forced into hypocritical efforts to prevent the fugitive ecclesiastic's pursuit, extradition, trial and imprisonment, and these efforts, despite their disingenuous character, succeeded. Under another name, he now preaches Christ and Him crucified in the far West, and is, we daresay, a leading advocate of Prohibition, vice-crusading and the other Methodist reforms.

But here we depart from the point. It is not that an eminent Wesleyan should be taken in crim. con. with a member of the Y. M. C. A.; it is that the whole Wesleyan scheme of things, despite the enormous multiplication of such incidents, should still stand above all direct and devastating criticism in America. It is an ignorant and dishonest cult of ignorant and dishonest men, and yet no one has

ever had at it from the front. All the newspaper clippings that we have mentioned were
extraordinarily discreet. Every offence of a
clergyman was presented as if it were an isolated
phenomenon, and of no general significance; there
was never any challenge of an ecclesiastical organization which bred and sheltered such men, and
carried over their curious ethics into its social and
political activities. That careful avoidance of the
main issue is always observable in These States.
Prohibition was saddled upon the country, against
the expressed wish of at least two-thirds of the
people, by the political chicanery of the same organization, and yet no one, during the long fight,
thought to attack it directly; to have done so would
have been to violate the taboo described. So when
the returning soldiers began to reveal the astounding chicaneries of the Young Men's Christian Association; it was marvelled at for a few weeks, as
Americans always marvel at successful pocket-
squeezings, but no one sought the cause in the character of the pious brethren primarily responsible.
And so, again, when what is called liberal opinion
began to revolt against the foreign politics of Dr.
Wilson, and in particular, against his apparent re-

[49]

pudiation of his most solemn engagements, and his complete insensibility, in the presence of a moral passion, to the most elementary principles of private and public honour. A thousand critics, friendly and unfriendly, sought to account for his amazing shifts and evasions on unintelligible logical grounds, but no one, so far as we know, ventured to point out that 'his course could be accounted for in every detail, and without any mauling of the facts whatsoever, upon the simple ground that he was a Presbyterian.

We sincerely hope that no one will mistake us here for anarchists who seek to hold the Presbyterian code of ethics, or the Presbyterians themselves, up to derision. We confess frankly that, .as private individuals, we are inclined against that code and that all our prejudices run against those who subscribe to it—which is to say, in the direction of toleration, of open dealing, and even of a certain mild snobbishness. We are both opposed to moral enthusiasm, and never drink with a moral man if it can be avoided. The taboos that we personally subscribe to are taboos upon the very things that Presbyterians hold most dear—for example, moral certainty, the proselyting appetite, and what

[50]

may be described as the passion of the policeman. But we are surely not fatuous enough to cherish our ideas to the point of fondness. In the long run, we freely grant, it may turn out that the Presbyterians are right and we are wrong—in brief, that God loves a moral man more than he loves an amiable and honourable one. Stranger things, indeed, have happened; one might even argue without absurdity that God is actually a Presbyterian Himself. Whether He is or is not we do not presume to say; we simply record the fact that it is our present impression that He is not—and then straightway admit that our view is worth no more than that of any other pair of men.

Meanwhile, however, it is certainly not going too far to notice the circumstance that there is an irreconcilable antithesis between the two sorts of men that we have described—that a great moral passion is fatal to the gentler and more caressing amenities of life, and *vice versa*. The man of morals has a certain character, and the man of honour has a quite different character. No one not an idiot fails to differentiate between the two, or to order his intercourse with them upon an assumption of their disparity. What we know in the

[51]

United States as a Presbyterian is pre-eminently of the moral type. Perhaps more than any other man among us he regulates his life, and the lives of all who fall under his influence, upon a purely moral plan. In the main, he gets the principles underlying that plan from the Old Testament; if he is to be described succinctly, it is as one who carries over into modern life, with its superior complexity of sin, the simple and rigid ethical concepts of the ancient Jews. And in particular, he subscribes to their theory that it is virtuous to make things hot for the sinner, by which word he designates any person whose conduct violates the ordinances of God as he himself is aware of them and interprets them. Sin is to the Presbyterian the salient phenomenon of this wobbling and nefarious world, and the pursuit and chastisement of sinners the one avocation that is permanently worth while. The product of that simple doctrine is a character of no little vigour and austerity, and one much esteemed by the great masses of men, who are always uneasily conscious of their own weakness in the face of temptation and thus have a sneaking veneration for the man apparently firm, and who are always ready to believe, furthermore, that any man who

[52]

seems to be having a pleasant time is a rascal and deserving of the fire.

The Presbyterian likewise harbours this latter suspicion. More, he commonly erects it into a certainty. Every single human act, he holds, must be either right or wrong—and the overwhelming majority of them are wrong. He knows exactly what these wrong ones are; he recognizes them instantly and infallibly, by a sort of inspired intuition; and he believes that they should all be punished automatically and with the utmost severity. No one ever heard of a Presbyterian overlooking a fault, or pleading for mercy for the erring. He would regard such an act as the weakness of one ridden by the Devil. From such harsh judgments and retributions, it must be added in fairness, he does not except himself. He detects his own aberration almost as quickly as he detects the aberration of the other fellow, and though he may sometimes seek—being, after all, only human —to escape its consequences, he by no means condones it. Nothing, indeed, could exceed the mental anguish of a Presbyterian who has been betrayed, by the foul arts of some lascivious wench, into any form of adultery, or, by the treason of his senses

[53]

in some other way, into a voluptuous yielding to
the lure of the other *beaux arts*. It has been our
fortune, at various times, to be in the confidence
of Presbyterians thus seduced from their native
virtue, and we bear willing testimony to their sincere horror. Even the least pious of them was as
greatly shaken up by what to us, on our lower plane,
seemed a mere peccadillo, perhaps in bad taste.
but certainly not worth getting into a sweat about,
as we ourselves would have been by a gross breach
of faith.

But, as has been before remarked, the bitter
must go with the sweet. In the face of so exalted a moral passion it would be absurd to look for
that urbane habit which seeks the well-being of
one's self and the other fellow, not in exact
obedience to harsh statutes, but in ease, dignity and
the more delicate sort of self-respect. That is to
say, it would be absurd to ask a thoroughly moral
man to be also a man of honour. The two, in fact,
are eternal enemies; their endless struggle achieves
that happy mean of philosophies which we call
civilization. The man of morals keeps order in
the world, regimenting its lawless hordes and organ-
izing its governments; the man of honour mellows

[54]

and embellishes what is thus achieved, giving to duty the aspect of a privilege and making human intercourse a thing of fine faiths and understandings. We trust the former to do what is righteous; we trust the latter to do what is seemly. It is seldom that a man can do both. The man of honour inevitably exalts the punctilio above the law of God; one may trust him, if he has eaten one's salt, to respect one's daughter as he would his own, but if he happens to be under no such special obligation it may be hazardous to trust him with even one's charwoman or one's mother-in-law. And the man of morals, confronted by a moral situation, is usually wholly without honour. Put him on the stand to testify against a woman, and he will tell all he knows about her, even including what he has learned in the purple privacy of her boudoir. More, he will not tell it reluctantly, shame-facedly, apologetically, but proudly and willingly, in response to his high sense of moral duty. It is simply impossible for such a man to lie like a gentleman. He lies, of course, like all of us, and perhaps more often than most of us on the other side, but he does it, not to protect sinners from the moral law, but to make their punishment under the

[55]

moral law more certain, swift, facile and spectacular.

By this long route we get at our *apologia* for Dr. Wilson, a man from whom we both differ in politics, in theology, in ethics and in epistemology, but one whose great gifts, particularly for moral endeavour in the grand manner, excite our sincere admiration. Both his foes and his friends, it seems to us, do him a good deal of injustice. The former, carried away by that sense of unlikeness which lies at the bottom of most of the prejudices of uncritical men, denounce him out of hand because he is not as they are. A good many of these foes, of course, are not actually men of honour themselves; some of them, in fact, belong to sects and professions— for example, that of intellectual Socialist and that of member of Congress—in which no authentic man of honour could imaginably have a place. But it may be accurately said of them, nevertheless, that if actual honour is not in them, then at least they have something of the manner of honour—that they are moving in the direction of honour, though not yet arrived. Few men, indeed, may be said to belong certainly and irrevocably in either category, that of the men of honour or that of the men of

[56]

morals. Dr. Wilson, perhaps, is one such man. He is as palpably and exclusively a man of morals as, say, George Washington was a man of honour. He is, in the one category, a great beacon, burning almost blindingly; he is, in the other, no more than a tallow dip, guttering asthmatically. But the majority of men occupy a sort of twilight zone, and the most that may be said of them is that their faces turn this way or that. Such is the case with Dr. Wilson's chief foes. Their eyes are upon honour, as upon some new and superlatively sweet enchantment, and, bemused to starboard, they view the scene to port with somewhat extravagant biliousness. Thus, when they contemplate His Excellency's long and perhaps unmatchable series of violations of his troth—in the matter of "keeping us out of the war," in the matter of his solemn promises to China, in the matter of his statement of war aims and purposes, in the matter of his shifty dealing with the Russian question, in the matter of his repudiation of the armistice terms offered to the Germans, in the matter of his stupendous lying to the Senate committee on foreign relations, and so on, *ad infinitum*—when they contemplate all that series of evasions, dodgings, hypocrisies, double-

[57]

dealings and plain mendacities, they succumb to an indignation that is still more than half moral, and denounce him bitterly as a Pecksniff, a Tartuffe and a Pinto. In that judgment, as we shall show, there is naught save a stupid incapacity to understand an unlike man—in brief, no more than the dunderheadedness which makes a German regard every Englishman as a snuffling poltroon, hiding behind his vassals, and causes an Englishman to look upon every German as a fiend in human form, up to his hips in blood.

But one expects a man's foes to misjudge him, and even to libel him deliberately; a good deal of their enmity, in fact, is often no more than a product of their uneasy consciousness that they have dealt unfairly with him; one is always most bitter, not toward the author of one's wrongs, but toward the victim of one's wrongs. Unluckily, Dr. Wilson's friends have had at him even more cruelly. When, seeking to defend what they regard as his honour, they account for his incessant violation of his pledges—to the voters in 1916, to the soldiers drafted for the war, to the Chinese on their entrance, to the Austrians when he sought to get them out, to the Germans when he offered them his four-

[58]

teen points, to the country in the matter of secret diplomacy—when his friends attempt to explain his cavalier repudiation of all these pledges on the ground that he could not have kept them without violating later pledges, they achieve, of course, only an imbecility, obvious and damning, for it must be plain that no man is permitted, in honour, to make antagonistic engagements, or to urge his private tranquillity or even the public welfare as an excuse for changing their terms without the consent of the parties of the second part. A man of honour is one who simply does whatever he says he will do, provided the other party holds to the compact too. One cannot imagine him shifting, trimming and making excuses; it is his peculiar mark that he never makes excuses—that the need of making them would fill him with unbearable humiliation. The moment a man of honour faces the question of his honour, he is done for; it can no more stand investigation than the chastity of a woman can stand investigation. In such a character, Dr. Wilson would have been bound irrevocably by all his long series of solemn engagements, from the first to the last, without the slightest possibility of dotting an i or of cutting off the tail of a comma. It would have

[59]

been as impossible for him to have repudiated a single one of them at the desire of his friends or in the interest of his idealistic enterprises as it would have been for him to have repudiated it to his own private profit.

But here is where both foes and friends go aground; both attempt to inject concepts of honour into transactions predominatingly, and perhaps exclusively, coloured by concepts of morals. The two things are quite distinct, as the two sorts of men are quite distinct. Beside the obligation of honour there is the obligation of morals, entirely independent and often directly antagonistic. And beside the man who yields to the punctilio—the man of honour, the man who keeps his word—there is the man who submits himself, regardless of his personal engagements and the penalties that go therewith, to the clarion call of the moral law. Dr. Wilson is such a man. He is, as has been remarked, a Presbyterian, a Calvinist, a militant moralist. In that rôle, devoted to that high cause, clad in that white garment, he was purged of all obligations of honour to any merely earthly power. His one obligation was to the moral law—in brief, to the ordinance of God, as determined by Chris-

[60]

tian pastors. Under that moral law, specifically, he was charged to search out and determine its violations by the accused in the dock, to wit, by the German nation, according to the teaching of those pastors and the light within, and to fix and execute a punishment that should be swift, terrible and overwhelming.

To this business, it must be granted by even his most extravagant opponents, he addressed himself with the loftiest resolution and singleness of purpose, excluding all puerile questions of ways and means. He was, by the moral law, no more bound to take into account the process whereby the accused was brought to book and the weight of retribution brought to bear than a detective is bound to remember how any ordinary prisoner is snared for the mill of justice. The detective himself may have been an important factor in that process; he may have taken the prisoner by some stratagem involving the most gross false pretences; he may have even played the *agent provocateur* and so actually suggested, planned and supervised the crime. But surely that would be a ridiculous critic who would argue thereby that the detective should forthwith forget the law violated and the punishment justly

[61]

provided for it, and go over to the side of the defence on the ground that his dealings with the prisoner involved him in obligations of honour. The world would laugh at such a moral moron, if it did not actually destroy him as an enemy of society. It recognizes the two codes that we have described, and it knows that they are antagonistic. It expects a man sworn to the service of morality to discharge his duty at any cost to his honour, just as it expects a man publicly devoted to honour to keep his word at any cost to his or to the public morals. Moreover, it inclines, when there is a conflict, toward the side of morals; the overwhelming majority of men are men of morals, not men of honour. They believe that it is vastly more important that the guilty should be detected, taken into custody and exposed to the rigour of the law than that the honour of this or that man should be preserved. In truth, there are frequent circumstances under which they positively esteem a man who thus sacrifices his honour, or even their own honour. The man of *dis*honour may actually take on the character of a public hero. Thus, in 1903, when the late Major General Roosevelt, then President, tore up the treaty of 1846, whereby the United

States guaranteed the sovereignty of Columbia in the Isthmus of Panama, the great masses of the American plain people not only at once condoned this grave breach of honour, but actually applauded Dr. Roosevelt because his act furthered the great moral enterprise of digging the canal.

These distinctions, of course, are familiar to all men who devote themselves to the study of the human psyche; that morals and honour are not one and the same thing, but two very distinct and even antithetical things, is surely no news to the judicious. But what is thus merely an axiom of ethics, politics or psychology is often kept strangely secret in the United States. We have acquired the habit of evading all the facts of life save those that are most superficial; by long disuse we have almost lost the capacity for thinking analytically and accurately. A thing may be universally known among us, and yet never get itself so much as mentioned. Around scores of elementary platitudes there hangs a shuddering silence as complete as that which hedges in the sacred name of a Polynesian chief. At every election time, in our large cities, most of the fundamental issues are concealed, particularly when they happen to take on a theological colour, which is very often. It is, for example, the timorous public theory, born of this fear of the forthright fact, that when a man sets up as a candidate for, say, a judgeship, the question of his private religious faith is of no practical importance— that it makes no difference whether he is a Catholic or a Methodist. The truth is, of course, that his faith is often of the very first importance—that it will colour his conduct of the forensic combats before him even more than his politics, his capacity to digest proteids or the social aspirations of his wife. One constantly notes, in American jurisprudence, the effects of theological prejudices on the bench; there are at least a dozen controlling decisions, covering especially the new moral legislation, which might almost be mistaken by a layman for sermons by the Rev. Dr. Billy Sunday. The Prohibitionists, during their long and very adroit campaign, shrewdly recognized the importance of controlling the judiciary; in particular, they threw all their power against the election of candidates who were known to be Catholics, or Jews, or freethinkers. As a result they packed the bench of nearly every state with Methodist, Baptist and Presbyterian judges, and these gentlemen at once up-

[64]

held all their maze of outrageous statutes. That they would do so if elected was known in advance, and yet, so far as the record shows, it was a rare thing for any one to attack them on the ground of their religion, and rarer still for any such attack to influence many votes. The taboo was working. The majority of voters were eager to avoid that issue. They felt, in some vague and unintelligible way, that it was improper to raise it.

So with all other primary issues. There is surely no country in the world in which the marriage relation is discussed more copiously than in the United States, and yet there is no country in which its essentials are more diligently avoided. Some years ago, seeking to let some sagacity into the prevailing exchange of platitudes, one of us wrote a book upon the subject, grounding it upon the obvious doctrine that women have much more to gain by marriage than men, and that the majority of men are aware of it, and would never marry at all if it were not for women's relentless effort to bring them to it. This banality the writer supported, by dint of great painstaking, in a somewhat novel way. That is to say, he put upon himself the limitation of employing no theory, statement of fact

[65]

or argument in the book that was not already embodied in a common proverb in some civilized language. Now and then it was a bit hard to find the proverb, but in most cases it was very easy, and in some cases he found, not one, but dozens. Well, this laborious *pastiche* of the obvious made such a sensation that it sold better than any other book that the author had ever written—and the reviews unanimously described it, either with praise or with blame, as an extraordinary collection of heresies, most of them almost too acrid to be bruited about. In other words, this mass of platitudes took Americans by surprise, and somehow shocked them. What was commonplace to even the peasants of the European Continent was so unfamiliar to even the literate minority over here that the book acquired a sort of sinister repute, and the writer himself came to be discussed as a fellow with the habit of arising in decorous society and indelicately blowing his nose.

There is, of course, something of the same shrinking from the elemental facts of life in England; it seems to run with the Anglo-Saxon. This accounts for the shuddering attitude of the English to such platitude-monging foreigners as George Bernard

[66]

Shaw, the Scotsman disguised as an Irishman, and
G. K. Chesterton, who shows all the physical and
mental stigmata of a Bavarian. Shaw's plays,
which once had all England by the ears, were set
down as compendiums of the self-evident by the
French, a realistic and plain-spoken people, and
were sniffed at in Germany by all save the middle
classes, who correspond to the *intelligentsia* of
Anglo-Saxondom. But in America, even more than
in England, they were viewed as genuinely satanic.
We shall never forget, indeed, the tremulous manner in which American audiences first listened to
the feeble rattling of the palpable in such pieces as
"Man and Superman" and "You Never Can Tell."
It was precisely the manner of an old maid devour-
ing "What Every Girl of Forty-Five Should Know"
behind the door. As for Chesterton, his banal ar-
guments in favour of alcohol shocked the country
so greatly that his previous high services to religious superstition were forgotten, and today he is
seldom mentioned by respectable Americans.

v

It is necessary to repeat that we rehearse all these
facts, not in indignation, nor indeed in any spirit

of carping whatever, but in perfect serenity and simply as descriptive sociologists. This attitude of mind is but little comprehended in America, where the emotions dominate all human reactions, and even such dismal sciences as paleontology, pathology and comparative philology are gaudily coloured by patriotic and other passions. The typical American learned man suffers horribly from the national disease: he is eternally afraid of something. If it is not that some cheese-monger among his trustees will have him cashiered for receiving a picture post-card from Prof. Dr. Scott Nearing, it is that some sweating and scoundrelly German or Frenchman will discover and denounce his cribs, and if it is not that the foreigner will have at him, it is that he will be robbed of his step from associate to full professor by some rival whose wife is more amiable to the president of the university, or who is himself more popular with the college athletes. Thus surrounded by fears, he translates them, by a familiar psychological process, into indignations. He announces what he has to say in terms of raucous dudgeon, as a negro, having to go past a medical college at night, intones some bellicose gospel-hymn. He is, in brief, vociferously correct. During the late war, at a time of unusual suspicions and hence of unusual hazards, this eagerness to prove orthodoxy by choler was copiously on exhibition. Thus one of the leading American zoölogists printed a work in which, after starting off by denouncing the German naming of new species as ignorant, dishonest and against God, he gradually worked himself up to the doctrine that any American who put a tooth into a slab of *Rinderbrust mit Meerrettig,* or peeped at *Simplicissimus* with the blinds down, or bought his children German-made jumping-jacks, was a traitor to the Constitution and a secret agent of the Wilhelmstrasse. And thus there were American pathologists and bacteriologists who denounced Prof. Dr. Paul Ehrlich as little better than a quack hired by the Krupps to poison Americans, and who displayed their pious horror of the late Prof. Dr. Robert Koch by omitting all acknowledgment of obligation to him from their monographs. And finally there was the posse of "two thousand American Historians" assembled by Mr. Creel to instruct the plain people in the new theory of American history, whereby the Revolution was represented as a lamentable row in an otherwise happy family, delib-

[69]

erately instigated by German intrigue—a posse which reached its greatest height of correct indignation in its approval of the celebrated Sisson documents, to the obscene delight of the British authors thereof.

As we say, we are devoid of all such lofty passions, and hence must present our observations in the flat, unimaginative, unemotional manner of a dentist pulling a tooth. It would not be going too far, in fact, to call us emotional idiots. What ails us is a constitutional suspicion that the other fellow, after all, may be right, or, in any event, partly right. In the present case we by no means reprehend the avoidance of issues that we have described; we merely record it. The fact is that it has certain very obvious uses, and is probably inevitable in a democratic society. It is commonly argued that free speech is necessary to the prosperity of a democracy, but in this doctrine we take no stock. On the contrary, there are plain reasons for holding that free speech is more dangerous to a democracy than to any other form of government, and no doubt these reasons, if only unconsciously, were at the bottom of the extraordinary body of repressive legislation put upon the books

[70]

during the late war. The essential thing about a democracy is that the men at the head of the state are wholly dependent, for a continuance of their power, upon the good opinion of the popular majority. While they are actually in office, true enough, they are theoretically almost completely irresponsible, but their terms of office are usually so short that they must give constant thought to the imminent canvassing of their acts, and this threat of being judged and turned out commonly greatly conditions their exercise of their power, even while they hold it to the full. Of late, indeed, there has actually arisen the doctrine that they are responsible at all times and must respond to every shift in public sentiment, regardless of their own inclinations, and there has even grown up the custom of subjecting them to formal discipline, as by what is called the recall. The net result is that a public officer under a democracy is bound to regard the popular will during the whole of his term in office, and cannot hope to carry out any intelligible plan of his own if the mob has been set against it.

Now, the trouble with this scheme is that the mob reaches its conclusions, not by logical steps

[71]

but by emotional steps, and that its information upon all save a very small minority of the questions publicly at issue is always scant and inaccurate. It is thus constantly liable to inflammation by adroit demagogues, or rabble-rousers, and inasmuch as these rabble-rousers are animated as a sole motive by the hope of turning out the existing officers of state and getting the offices for themselves, the man in office must inevitably regard them as his enemies and the doctrines they preach as subversive of good government. This view is not altogether selfish. There is, in fact, sound logic in it, for it is a peculiarity of the mob mind that it always takes in most hospitably what is intrinsically most idiotic—that between two antagonistic leaders it always follows the one who is longest on vague and brilliant words and shortest on sense. Thus the man in office, if he would be free to carry on his duties in anything approaching freedom and comfort, must adopt measures against that tendency to run amuck.

Three devices at once present themselves. One is to take steps against the rabble-rousers by seeking to make it appear that they are traitors, and so arousing the mob against them—in brief, to deny them their constitutional right to free speech under colour of criminal statutes. The second is to combine this plan with that of flooding the country with official news by a corps of press-agents, chautauquans and other such professors of deception. The third is to meet the rabble-rousers on their own ground, matching their appeals to the emotions with appeals even more powerful, and outdoing their vague and soothing words with words even more vague and soothing. All three plans have been in operation since the first days of the republic; the early Federalists employed the first two with such assiduity that the mob of that time finally revolted. All three were brought to the highest conceivable point of perfection by the late Dr. Wilson, a man whose resolute fidelity to his moral ideas was matched only by his magnificent skill at playing upon every prejudice and weakness of the plain people.

But men of such exalted and varied gifts are not common. The average head of a democratic state is not *ipso facto* the best rabble-rouser within that state, but merely one of the best. He may be able, on fair terms, to meet any individual rival, but it is rare for him to be able to meet the whole pack,

[73]

or even any considerable group. To relieve him from that difficulty, and so prevent the incessant running amuck of the populace, it is necessary to handicap all the remaining rabble-rousers, and this is most effectively done by limitations upon free speech which originate as statutes and gradually take on the form and potency of national customs. Such limitations arose in the United States by precisely that process. They began in the first years of the republic as definite laws. Some of those laws were afterward abandoned, but what was fundamentally sound in them remained in force as custom.

It must be obvious that even Dr. Wilson, despite his tremendous gift for the third of the devices that we have named, would have been in sore case during his second administration if it had not been for his employment of the other two. Imagine the United States during the Summer of 1917 with absolute free speech the order of the day! The mails would have been flooded with Socialist and pacifist documents, every street-corner would have had its screaming soap-box orator, the newspapers would have shaken the very heavens with colossal alarms, and conscientious objection would have taken on the proportions of a national frenzy. In the face of such an avalanche of fears and balderdash, there would have been no work at all for the German propagandists; in fact, it is likely that a great many of them, under suspicion on account of their relative moderation, would have been lynched as agents of the American munitions patriots. For the mob, it must be remembered, infallibly inclines, not to the side of the soundest logic and loftiest purpose, but to the side of the loudest noise, and without the artificial aid of a large and complex organization of press-agents and the power to jail any especially effective opponent forthwith, even a President of the United States would be unable to bawl down the whole fraternity. That it is matter of the utmost importance, in time of war, to avoid any such internal reign of terror must be obvious to even the most fanatical advocate of free speech. There must be, in such emergencies, a resolute pursuit of coherent policies, and that would be obviously impossible with the populace turning distractedly to one bogus messiah after another, and always seeking to force its latest craze upon the government. Thus, while one may perchance drop a tear or two upon the Socialists jailed by a sort of

[75]

lynch law for trying to exercise their plain constitutional rights, and upon the pacifists tarred and
feathered by mobs led by government agents, and
upon the conscientious objectors starved and
clubbed to death in military dungeons, it must still
be plain that such barbarous penalties were essen-
tially necessary. The victims, in the main, were
half-wits suffering from the martyr complex; it
was their admitted desire to sacrifice themselves for
the Larger Good. This desire was gratified—not
in the way they hoped for, of course, but nevertheless in a way that must have given any impartial
observer a feeling of profound, if discreditable,
satisfaction.

What a republic has to fear especially is the
rabble-rouser who advocates giving an objective
reality to the gaudy theories which lie at the foundations of the prevailing scheme of government. He
is far more dangerous than a genuine revolutionist,
for the latter comes with ideas that are actually new,
or, at all events, new to the mob, and so he has to
overcome its congenital hostility to novelty. But
the reformer who, under a democracy, bases his
case upon the principles upon which democracy is
founded has an easy road, for the populace is

familiar with those principles and eager to see them put into practical effect. The late Cecil Chesterton, in his penetrating "History of the United States," showed how Andrew Jackson came to power by that route. Jackson, he said, was simply a man so naïve that he accepted the lofty doctrines of the Declaration of Independence without any critical questioning whatever, and "really acted as if they were true." The appearance of such a man, he goes on, was "appalling" to the political aristocrats of 1825. They themselves, of course, enunciated those doctrines daily and based their whole politics upon them—but not to the point of really executing them. So when Jackson came down from the mountains with the same sonorous words upon his lips, but with the addition of a solemn promise to carry them out—when he thus descended upon them, he stole their thunder and spiked their guns, and after a brief struggle he had disposed of them. The Socialists, free-speech fanatics, anti-conscriptionists, anti-militarists and other such democratic maximalists of 1917 and 1918 were, in essence, nothing but a new and formidable horde of Jacksons. Their case rested upon principles held to be true by all good Ameri-

[77]

cans, and constantly reaffirmed by the highest officers of state. It was thus extremely likely that, if they were permitted to woo the public ear, they would quickly amass a majority of suffrages, and so get the conduct of things into their own hands. So it became necessary, in order that the great enterprises then under way might be pushed to a successful issue, that all these marplots be silenced, and it was accordingly done. This proceeding, of course, was theoretically violative of their common rights, and hence theoretically un-American. All the theory, in fact, was on the side of the victims. But war time is no time for theories, and a man with war powers in his hands is not one to parley with them.

As we have said, the menace presented by such unintelligent literalists is probably a good deal more dangerous to a democracy than to a government of any other form. Under an aristocracy, for example, such as prevailed, in one form or another, in England, Germany, Italy and France before the war, it is possible to give doctrinaires a relatively free rein, for even if they succeed in converting the mob to their whim-wham, there remain insuperable impediments to its adoption and execution as law. In England, as every one knows, the impediment was a ruling caste highly skilled in the governmental function and generally trusted by a majority of the populace—a ruling caste firmly intrenched in the House of Lords and scarcely less powerful in the House of Commons. In France it was a bureaucracy so securely protected by law and custom that nothing short of a political cataclysm could shake it. In Germany and Italy it was an aristocracy buttressed by laws cunningly designed to nullify the numerical superiority of the mob, and by a monarchical theory that set up a heavy counter-weight to public opinion.

In the face of such adroit checks and balances it is a matter of relative indifference whether the mob blows scalding hot or freezing cold. Whatever the extravagance of its crazes, there remains effective machinery for holding them in check until they spend themselves, which is usually soon enough. Thus the English government, though theoretically as much opposed to anarchists as the American government, gave them cheerful asylum before the war and permitted them to preach their lamentable notions almost without check, whereas in America they early aroused great fears and

[79]

were presently put under such disabilities that their propaganda became almost impossible. Even in France, where they had many converts and were frequently in eruption, there was far more hospitality to them than in the United States. And thus in the Germany of Bismarck's day, the Socialists, after a brief and aberrant attempt to suppress them, were allowed to run free, despite the fact that their doctrine was quite as abhorrent to German official doctrine as anarchism was to American official doctrine. The German ruling caste of those days was sheltered behind laws and customs which enabled it to pull the teeth of Socialism, even in the face of enormous Socialist majorities. But under a democracy it is difficult, and often downright impossible, to oppose the popular craze of the moment with any effect, and so there must be artificial means of disciplining the jake-fetchers who seek to set such enthusiasms in motion. The shivering fear of Bolshevism, visible of late among the capitalists of America, is based upon a real danger. These capitalists have passed through the burning fires of Rooseveltian trust-busting and Bryanistic populism, and they know very well that half a dozen Lenines and Trotskis, turned loose upon the plain

[80]

people, would quickly recruit a majority of them for a holy war upon capital, and that they have the political power to make such a holy war devastating.

The amateur of popular psychology may wonder why it is that the mob, in the face of the repressions constantly practised in the United States, does not occasionally rise in revolt, and so get back its right to be wooed and ravished by all sorts of mountebanks. Theoretically it has that right, and what is more, it has the means of regaining it; nothing could resist it if it made absolute free speech an issue in a national campaign and voted for the candidate advocating it. But something is overlooked here, and that is the fact that the mob has no liking for free speech *per se*. Some of the grounds of its animosity we have rehearsed. Others are not far to seek. One of them lies in the mob's chronic suspicion of all advocates of ideas, born of its distaste for ideas themselves. The mobman cannot imagine himself throwing up his job and deserting his home, his lodge and his speakeasy to carry a new gospel to his fellows, and so he is inclined to examine the motives of any other man who does so. The one motive that is intelligible to him is the desire for profit, and he commonly con-

[81]

cludes at once that this is what moves the propagandist before him. His reasoning is defective, but his conclusion is usually not far from right. In point of fact, idealism is not a passion in America, but a trade; all the salient idealists make a living at it, and some of them, for example, Dr. Bryan and the Rev. Dr. Sunday, are commonly believed to have amassed large fortunes. For an American to advocate a cause without any hope of private usufruct is almost unheard of; it would be difficult to find such a man who was not plainly insane. The most eloquent and impassioned of American idealists are candidates for public office; on the lower levels idealism is no more than a handmaiden of business, like advertising or belonging to the Men and Religion Forward Movement.

Another and very important cause of the proletarian's failure to whoop for free speech is to be found in his barbarous delight in persecution, regardless of the merits of the cause. The spectacle of a man exercising the right of free speech yields, intrinsically, no joy, for there is seldom anything dramatic about it. But the spectacle of a man being mobbed, jailed, beaten and perhaps murdered for trying to exercise it is a good show like any

[82]

other good show, and the populace is thus not only eager to witness it but even willing to help it along. It is therefore quite easy to set the mob upon, say, the Bolsheviki, despite the fact that the Bolsheviki have the professed aim of doing the mob an incomparable service. During the war-time jinks of the Postoffice and the Department of Justice, popular opinion was always on the side of the raiding parties. It applauded every descent upon a Socialist or pacifist meeting, not because it was very hotly in favour of war—in fact, it was lukewarm about war, and resisted all efforts to heat it up until overwhelming swarms of yokel-yankers were turned upon it—but because it was in favour of a safe and stimulating form of rough-house, with the police helping instead of hindering. It never stopped to inquire about the merits of the matter. All it asked for was a melodramatic raid, followed by a noisy trial of the accused in the newspapers, and the daily publication of sensational (and usually bogus) evidence about the discovery of compromising literature in his wife's stockings, including records of his receipt of $100,000 from von Bernstorff, Carranza or some other transient hobgoblin. The celebrated O'Leary trial was typical. After months of

blood-curdling charges in the press, it turned out
when the accused got before a court that the evidence against him, on which it was sought to convict him of a capital offence, was so feeble that it
would have scarcely sufficed to convict him of an
ordinary misdemeanor, and that most of this feeble
testimony was palpably perjured. Nevertheless,
public opinion was nearly unanimously against him
from first to last, and the jury which acquitted him
was almost apologetic about its inability to give the
populace the crowning happiness of a state hanging.

Under cover of the war, of course, the business
of providing such shows prospered extraordinarily,
but it is very active even in time of peace. The surest way to get on in politics in America is to play the
leading part in a prosecution which attracts public
notice. The list of statesmen who have risen in
that fashion includes the names of many of the
highest dignity, *e. g.*, Hughes, Folk, Whitman,
Heney, Baker and Palmer. Every district attorney
in America prays nightly that God will deliver
into his hands some Thaw, or Becker, or O'Leary,
that he may get upon the front pages and so become
a governor, a United States senator, or a justice of
the Supreme Court of the United States. The late

[84]

crusade against W. R. Hearst, which appeared to the public as a great patriotic movement, was actually chiefly managed by a subordinate prosecuting officer who hoped to get high office out of it.

This last aspirant failed in his enterprise largely because he had tackled a man who was himself of superb talents as a rouser of the proletariat, but nine times out of ten the thing succeeds. Its success is due almost entirely to the factor that we have mentioned, to wit, to the circumstance that the sympathy of the public is always on the side of the prosecution. This sympathy goes so far that it is ready to condone the most outrageous conduct in judges and prosecuting officers, providing only they give good shows. During the late war upon Socialists, pacifists, anti-conscriptionists and other such heretics, judges theoretically employed to insure fair trials engaged in the most amazing attacks upon prisoners before them, denouncing them without hearing them, shutting out evidence on their side and making stump speeches to the jury against them. That conduct aroused no public indignation; on the contrary, such judges were frequently praised in the newspapers and a good many of them were promoted to higher courts. Even in

[85]

time of peace there is no general antipathy to that sort of thing. At least two-thirds of our judges, federal, state and municipal, colour their decisions with the newspaper gabble of the moment; even the Supreme Court has shown itself delicately responsive to the successive manias of the Uplift, which is, at bottom, no more than an organized scheme for inventing new crimes and making noisy pursuit of new categories of criminals. Some time ago an intelligent Mexican, after studying our courts, told us that he was surprised that, in a land ostensibly of liberty, so few of the notorious newspaper-wooers and blacklegs upon the bench were assassinated. It is, in fact, rather curious. The thing happens very seldom, and then it is usually in the South, where the motive is not altruistic but political. That is to say, the assassin merely desires to remove one blackleg in order to make a place for some other blackleg. He has no objection to systematized injustice; all he desires is that it be dispensed in favour of his own side.

VI

The mob delight in melodramatic and cruel spectacles, thus constantly fed and fostered by the judicial arm in the United States, is also at the bottom of another familiar American phenomenon, to wit, lynching. A good part of the enormous literature of lynching is devoted to a discussion of its causes, but most of that discussion is ignorant and some of it is deliberately mendacious. The majority of Southern commentators argue that the motive of the lynchers is a laudable yearning to "protect Southern womanhood," despite the plain fact that only a very small proportion of the blackamoors hanged and burned are even so much as accused of molesting Southern womanhood. On the other hand, some of the negro intellectuals of the North ascribe the recurrent butcheries to the Southern white man's economic jealousy of the Southern black, who is fast acquiring property and reaching out for the prerogatives that go therewith. Finally, certain white Northerners seek a cause in mere political animosity, arguing that the Southern white hates the negro because the latter is his theoretical equal at the polls, though actually not permitted to vote.

All of these notions seem to us to be fanciful. Lynching is popular in the South simply because the Southern populace, like any other populace, delights in thrilling shows, and because no other sort of show is provided by the backward culture of the region. The introduction of prize-fighting down there, or baseball on a large scale, or amusement places like Coney Island, or amateur athletic contests, or picnics like those held by the more truculent Irish fraternal organizations, or any other such wholesale devices for shocking and diverting the proletariat would undoubtedly cause a great decline in lynching. The art is practised, in the overwhelming main, in remote and God-forsaken regions, in which the only rival entertainment is offered by one-sided political campaigns, third-rate chautauquas and Methodist revivals. When it is imitated in the North, it is always in some drab factory or mining town. Genuine race riots, of course, sometimes occur in the larger cities, but these are always economic in origin, and have nothing to do with lynching, properly so-called. One could not imagine an actual lynching at, say, Atlantic City, with ten or fifteen bands playing, blind pigs in operation up every alley, a theatre in every block or two, and the boardwalk swarming with ladies of joy. Even a Mississippian, transported to such scenes, succumbs to the atmosphere

[88]

of pleasure, and so has no seizures of moral rage against the poor darkey. Lynching, in brief, is a phenomenon of isolated and stupid communities, a mark of imperfect civilization; it follows the hookworm and malaria belt; it shows itself in inverse proportion to the number of shoot-the-chutes, symphony orchestras, roof gardens, theatres, horse races, yellow journals and automatic pianos. No one ever heard of a lynching in Paris, at Newport, or in London. But there are incessant lynchings in the remoter parts of Russia, in the backwoods of Serbia, Bulgaria and Herzegovina, in Mexico and Nicaragua, and in such barbarous American states as Alabama, Georgia and South Carolina.

The notion that lynching in the South is countenanced by the gentry or that they take an actual hand in it is libelous and idiotic. The well-born and well-bred Southerner is no more a savage than any other man of condition. He may live among savages, but that no more makes him a savage than an English gentleman is made one by having a place in Wales, or a Russian by living on his estate in the Ukraine. What Northern observers mistake for the gentry of the South, when they report the participation of "leading citizens" in a lynching, is

[89]

simply the office-holding and commercial bour-
geoisie—the offspring of the poor white trash who
skulked at home during the Civil War, robbing the
widows and orphans of the soldiers at the front,
and so laying the foundations of the present "industrial prosperity" of the section, *i. e.,* its con-
version from a region of large landed estates and
urbane life into a region of stinking factories,
filthy mining and oil towns, child-killing cotton
mills, vociferous chambers of commerce and other
such swineries. It is, of course, a fact that the
average lynching party in Mississippi or Alabama
is led by the mayor and that the town judge climbs
down from his bench to give it his official support,
but it is surely not a fact that these persons are of
the line of such earlier public functionaries as
Pickens, Troup and Pettus. On the contrary, they
correspond to the lesser sort of Tammany office-
holders and to the vermin who monopolize the public functions in such cities as Boston and Philadelphia. The gentry, with few exceptions, have
been forced out of the public service everywhere
south of the Potomac, if not out of politics. The
Democratic victory in 1912 flooded all the governmental posts at Washington with Southerners, and

some of them remain in office to this day, and are among the chief functionaries of the nation. But in the whole vast corps there are, we believe, but ten who would be accepted as gentlemen by Southern standards, and only three of these are in posts of any importance. In the two houses of Congress there is but one.

It is thus absurd to drag the gentry of the South—the Bourbons of New England legend—into a discussion of the lynching problem. They represent, in fact, what remains of the only genuine aristocracy ever visible in the United States, and lynching, on the theoretical side, is far too moral a matter ever to engage an aristocracy. The true lynchers are the plain people, and at the bottom of the sport there is nothing more noble than the mob man's chronic and ineradicable poltroonery. Cruel by nature, delighting in sanguinary spectacles, and here brought to hatred of the negro by the latter's increasing industrial, (*not* political, capitalistic or social) rivalry, he naturally diverts himself in his moments of musing with visions of what he would do to this or that Moor if he had the courage. Unluckily, he hasn't, and so he is unable to execute his dream *a cappella*. If, inflamed by

[91]

liquor, he attempts it, the Moor commonly gives
him a beating, or even murders him. But what
thus lies beyond his talents as an individual at once
becomes feasible when he joins himself with other
men in a like situation. This is the genesis of a
mob of lynchers. It is composed primarily of a
few men with definite grievances, sometimes against
the negro lynched but often against quite different
negroes. It is composed secondarily of a large
number of fifth-rate men eager for a thrilling show,
involving no personal danger. It is composed in
the third place of a few rabble-rousers and politicians, all of them hot to exhibit themselves before
the populace at a moment of public excitement and
in an attitude of leadership. It is the second ele-
ment that gives life to the general impulse. Without its ardent appetite for a rough and shocking
spectacle there would be no lynching. Its influence is plainly shown by the frequent unintelligi-
bility of the whole proceeding; all its indignation
over the crime alleged to be punished is an after-
thought; any crime will answer, once its blood is
up. Thus the most characteristic lynchings in the
South are not those in which a confessed criminal
is done to death for a definite crime, but those in

which, in sheer high spirits, some convenient African is taken at random and lynched, as the newspapers say, "on general principles." That sort of lynching is the most honest and normal, and we are also inclined to think that it is also the most enjoyable, for the other sort brings moral indignation with it, and moral indignation is disagreeable. No man can be both indignant and happy.

But here, seeking to throw a feeble beam or two of light into the mental processes of the American proletarian, we find ourselves entering upon a discussion that grows narrow and perhaps also dull. Lynching, after all, is not an American institution, but a peculiarly Southern institution, and even in the South it will die out as other more seemly recreations are introduced. It would be quite easy, we believe, for any Southern community to get rid of it by establishing a good brass band and having concerts every evening. It would be even easier to get rid of it by borrowing a few professional scoundrels from the Department of Justice, having them raid the "study" of the local Methodist archdeacon, and forthwith trying him publicly—with a candidate for governor as prosecuting officer—for seduction under promise of salvation. The trouble

[93]

down there is not a special viciousness. The Southern poor white, taking him by and large, is probably no worse and no better than the anthropoid proletarian of the North. What ails the whole region is Philistinism. It has lost its old aristocracy of the soil and has not yet developed an aristocracy of money. The result is that its cultural ideas are set by stupid and unimaginative men—Southern equivalents of the retired Iowa steer stuffers and grain sharks who pollute Los Angeles, American equivalents of the rich English nonconformists. These men, though they have accumulated wealth, have not yet acquired the capacity to enjoy civilized recreations. Worse, most of them are still so barbarous that they regard such recreations as immoral. The dominating opinion of the South is thus against most of the devices that would diminish lynching by providing substitutes for it. In every Southern town some noisy clown of a Methodist or Presbyterian clergyman exercises a local tyranny. These men are firmly against all the divertissements of more cultured regions. They oppose prize-fighting, horse-racing, Sunday baseball and games of chance. They are bitter prohibitionists. By their incessant vice-crusades

[94]

they reduce the romance of sex to furtiveness and piggishness. They know nothing of music or the drama, and view a public library merely as something to be rigorously censored. We are convinced that their ignorant moral enthusiasm is largely to blame for the prevalence of lynching. No doubt they themselves are sneakingly conscious of the fact, or at least aware of it subconsciously, for lynching is the only public amusement that they never denounce.

Their influence reveals strikingly the readiness of the inferior American to accept ready-made opinions. He seems to be pathetically eager to be told what to think, and he is apparently willing to accept any instructor who takes the trouble to tackle him. This, also, was brilliantly revealed during the late war. The powers which controlled the press during that fevered time swayed the populace as they pleased. So long as the course of Dr. Wilson was satisfactory to them he was depicted as a second Lincoln, and the plain people accepted the estimate without question. To help reinforce it the country was actually flooded with lithographs showing Lincoln and Wilson wreathed by the same branch of laurel, and copies of the print got into

[95]

millions of humble homes. But immediately Dr. Wilson gave offence to his superiors, he began to be depicted as an idiot and a scoundrel, and this judgment promptly displaced the other one in the popular mind. The late Major General Roosevelt was often a victim of that sort of boob-bumping. A man of mercurial temperament, constantly shifting his position on all large public questions, he alternately gave great joy and great alarm to the little group of sagaciously wilful men which exercises genuine sovereignty over the country, and this alternation of emotions showed itself, by way of the newspapers and other such bawdy agencies, in the vacillation of public opinion. The fundamental platitudes of the nation were used both for him and against him, and always with immense effect. One year he was the last living defender of the liberties fought for by the Fathers; the next year he was an anarchist. Roosevelt himself was much annoyed by this unreliability of the mob. Now and then he sought to overcome it by direct appeals, but in the long run he was usually beaten. Toward the end of his life he resigned himself to a policy of great discretion, and so withheld his voice until he was sure what hymn was being lined out.

The newspapers and press associations, of course, do not impart the official doctrine of the moment in terms of forthright instructions; they get it over, as the phrase is, in the form of delicate suggestions, most of them under cover of the fundamental platitudes aforesaid. Their job is not to inspire and inform public discussion, but simply to colour it, and the task most frequently before them is that of giving a patriotic and virtuous appearance to whatever the proletariat is to believe. They do this, of course, to the tune of deafening protestations of their own honesty and altruism. But there is really no such thing as an honest newspaper in America; if it were set up tomorrow it would perish within a month. Every journal, however rich and powerful, is the trembling slave of higher powers, some financial, some religious and some political. It faces a multitude of censorships, all of them very potent. It is censored by the Postoffice, by the Jewish advertisers, by the Catholic Church, by the Methodists, by the Prohibitionists, by the banking oligarchy of its town, and often by even more astounding authorities, including the Sinn Fein. Now and then a newspaper makes a valiant gesture of revolt, but it is only a gesture. There is not a

[97]

single daily in the United States that would dare to discuss the problem of Jewish immigration honestly. Nine tenths of them, under the lash of snobbish Jewish advertisers, are even afraid to call a Jew a Jew; their orders are to call him a Hebrew, which is regarded as sweeter. During the height of the Bolshevist scare not one American paper ventured to direct attention to the plain and obtrusive fact that the majority of Bolshevists in Russia and Germany and at least two-thirds of those taken in the United States were of the faith of Moses, Mendelssohn and Gimbel. But the Jews are perhaps not the worst. The Methodists, in all save a few big cities, exercise a control over the press that is far more rigid and baleful. In the Anti-Saloon League they have developed a machine for terrorizing office-holders and the newspapers that is remarkably effective, and they employed it during the long fight for Prohibition to throttle all opposition save the most formal.

In this last case, of course, the idealists who thus forced the speak-easy upon the country had an easy task, for all of the prevailing assumptions and prejudices of the mob were in their favour. No doubt it is true, as has been alleged, that a

[98]

majority of the voters of the country were against Prohibition and would have defeated it at a plebiscite, but equally without doubt a majority of them were against the politicians so brutally clubbed by the Anti-Saloon League, and ready to believe anything evil of them, and eager to see them manhandled. Moreover, the League had another thing in its favour: it was operated by strictly moral men, oblivious to any notion of honour. Thus it advocated and procured the abolition of legalized liquor selling without the slightest compensation to the men who had invested their money in the business under cover of and even at the invitation of the law—a form of repudiation and confiscation unheard of in any other civilized country. Again, it got through the constitutional amendment by promising the liquor men to give them one year to dispose of their lawfully accumulated stocks—and then broke its promise under cover of alleged war necessity, despite the fact that the war was actually over. Both proceedings, so abhorrent to any man of honour, failed to arouse any indignation among the plain people. On the contrary the plain people viewed them as, in some vague way, smart and creditable, and as, in any case, thoroughly justified by the superior moral obligation that we have hitherto discussed.

Thus the *Boobus americanus* is lead and watched over by zealous men, all of them highly skilled at training him in the way that he should think and act. The Constitution of his country guarantees that he shall be a free man and assumes that he is intelligent, but the laws and customs that have grown up under that Constitution give the lie to both the guarantee and the assumption. It is the fundamental theory of all the more recent American law, in fact, that the average citizen is half-witted, and hence not to be trusted to either his own devices or his own thoughts. If there were not regulations against the saloon (it seems to say) he would get drunk every day, dissipate his means, undermine his health and beggar his family. If there were not postal regulations as to his reading matter, he would divide his time between Bolshevist literature and pornographic literature and so become at once an anarchist and a guinea pig. If he were not forbidden under heavy penalites to cross a state line with a wench, he would be chronically unfaithful to his wife. Worse, if his daughter were not protected by statutes of the most draconian severity,

[100]

she would succumb to the first Italian she encountered, yield up her person to him, enroll herself upon his staff and go upon the streets. So runs the course of legislation in this land of freemen. We could pile up example upon example, but will defer the business for the present. Perhaps it may be resumed in a work one of us is now engaged upon—a full length study of the popular mind under the republic. But that work will take years. . . .

VII

No doubt we should apologize for writing, even so, so long a preface to so succinct a book. The one excuse we can think of is that, having read it, one need not read the book. That book, as we have said, may strike the superficial as jocular, but in actual fact it is a very serious and even profound composition, not addressed to the casual reader, but to the scholar. Its preparation involved a great diligence, and its study is not to be undertaken lightly. What the psychologist will find to admire in it, however, is not its learning and painstaking, its laborious erudition, but its compression. It establishes, we believe, a new and clearer method for a science long run to turgidity and flatulence. Perhaps it may be even said to set up an entirely new science, to wit, that of descriptive sociological psychology. We believe that this field will attract many men of inquiring mind hereafter and yield a valuable crop of important facts. The experimental method, intrinsically so sound and useful, has been much abused by orthodox psychologists; it inevitably leads them into a trackless maze of meaningless tables and diagrams; they keep their eyes so resolutely upon the intellectual process that they pay no heed to the primary intellectual materials. Nevertheless, it must be obvious that the conclusions that a man comes to, the emotions that he harbours and the crazes that sway him are of much less significance than the fundamental assumptions upon which they are all based.

There has been, indeed, some discussion of those fundamental assumptions of late. We have heard, for example, many acute discourses upon the effects produced upon the whole thinking of the German people, peasants and professors alike, by the underlying German assumption that the late Kaiser was anointed of God and hence above all ordinary human responsibility. We have heard talk, too, of the curious Irish axiom that there is a mysterious something in the nature of things, giving the Irish people an indefeasible right to govern Ireland as they please, regardless of the safety of their next-door neighbours. And we have heard many outlandish principles of the same sort from political theorists, *e. g.,* regarding the inalienable right of democracy to prevail over all other forms of government and the inalienable right of all national groups, however small, to self-determination. Well, here is an attempt to assemble in convenient form, without comment or interpretation, some of the fundamental beliefs of the largest body of human beings now under one flag in Christendom. It is but a beginning. The field is barely platted. It must be explored to the last furlong and all its fantastic and fascinating treasures unearthed and examined before ever there can be any accurate understanding of the mind of the American people.

GEORGE JEAN NATHAN
H. L. MENCKEN

New York, 1920.

[103]

THE AMERICAN CREDO

THE AMERICAN CREDO

§ 1

That the philoprogenitive instinct in rabbits is so intense that the alliance of two normally assiduous rabbits is productive of 265 offspring in one year.

§ 2

That there are hundreds of letters in the Dead Letter Office whose failure to arrive at their intended destinations was instrumental in separating as many lovers.

§ 3

That the Italian who sells bananas on a push-cart always takes the bananas home at night and sleeps with them under his bed.

§ 4

That a man's stability in the community and reliability in business may be measured by the number of children he has.

[107]

§ 5

That in Japan an American can buy a beautiful geisha for two dollars and that, upon being bought, she will promptly fall madly in love with him and will run his house for him in a scrupulously clean manner.

§ 6

That all sailors are gifted with an extraordinary propensity for amour, but that on their first night of shore leave they hang around the water-front blind-pigs and are given knock-out drops.

§ 7

That when a comedian, just before the rise of the curtain, is handed a telegram announcing the death of his mother or only child, he goes out on the stage and gives a more comic performance than ever.

§ 8

That the lions in the cage which a lion-tamer enters are always sixty years old and have had all their teeth pulled.

§ 9

That the Siamese Twins were joined together by

[108]

gutta percha moulded and painted to look like a shoulder blade.

§ 10

That if a woman about to become a mother plays the piano every day, her baby will be born a Victor Herbert.

§ 11

That all excursion boats are so old that if they ran into a drifting beer-keg they would sink.

§ 12

That a doctor knows so much about women that he can no longer fall in love with one of them.

§ 13

That when one takes one's best girl to see the monkeys in the zoo, the monkeys invariably do something that is very embarrassing.

§ 14

That firemen, awakened suddenly in the middle of the night, go to fires in their stocking feet.

§ 15

That something mysterious goes on in the rooms back of chop suey restaurants.

§ 16

That oil of pennyroyal will drive away mosquitoes.

§ 17

That the old ladies on summer hotel verandas devote themselves entirely to the discussion of scandals.

§ 18

That a bachelor, expecting a feminine visitor, by way of subtle preliminary strategy smells up his rooms with Japanese punk.

§ 19

That all one has to do to gather a large crowd in New York is to stand on the curb a few moments and gaze intently at the sky.

§ 20

That one can get an excellent bottle of wine in France for a franc.

[110]

That it is dangerous to drink out of a garden hose, since if one does one is likely to swallow a snake.

§ 22

That all male negroes can sing.

§ 23

That when a girl enters a hospital as a nurse, her primary object is always to catch one of the doctors.

§ 24

That the postmasters in small towns read all the postcards.

§ 25

That a young girl ought to devote herself sedulously to her piano lessons since, when she is married, her playing will be a great comfort to her husband.

§ 26

That all theater box-office employés are very impolite and hate to sell a prospective patron a ticket.

[111]

§ 27

That all great men have illegible signatures.

§ 28

That all iron-moulders and steam-fitters, back in the days of freedom, used to get drunk every Saturday night.

§ 29

That if a man takes a cold bath regularly every morning of his life he will never be ill.

§ 30

That ginger snaps are made of the sweepings of the floor in the bakery.

§ 31

That every circus clown's heart is breaking for one reason or another.

§ 32

That a bull-fighter always has so many women in love with him that he doesn't know what to do.

§ 33

That George M. Cohan spends all his time hanging around Broadway cafés and street-corners making flip remarks.

§ 34

That one can never tell accurately what the public wants.

§ 35

That every time one sat upon an old-fashioned horse-hair sofa one of the protruding sharp hairs would stab one through the union suit.

§ 36

That when an ocean vessel collides with another vessel or hits an iceberg and starts to sink, the ship's band promptly rushes up to the top deck and begins playing "Nearer, My God, to Thee."

§ 37

That in no town in America where it has played has "Uncle Tom's Cabin" ever failed to make money.

§ 38

That the tenement districts are the unhealthy places they are because the dwellers hang their bed-clothing out on the fire-escapes.

[113]

§ 39

That, in small town hotels, the tap marked "hot water" always gives forth cold water and that the tap marked "cold" always gives forth hot.

§ 40

That every lieutenant in the American army who went to France had an affair with a French comtesse.

§ 41

That when cousins marry, their children are born blind, deformed, or imbecile.

§ 42

That a cat falling from the twentieth story of the Singer Building will land upon the pavement below on its feet, uninjured and as frisky as ever.

§ 43

That the accumulation of great wealth always brings with it great unhappiness.

§ 44

That it is unlucky to count the carriages in a funeral.

§ 45

That the roulette wheel at Monte Carlo is controlled by a wire as thin as a hair which is controlled in turn by a button hidden beneath the rug near the operator's great toe.

§ 46

That Polish women are so little human that one of them can have a baby at 8 A. M. and cook her husband's dinner at noon.

§ 47

That Henry James never wrote a short sentence.

§ 48

That it is bad luck to kill a spider.

§ 49

That German peasants are possessed of a profound knowledge of music.

§ 50

That every coloured cook has a lover who never works, and that she feeds him by stealing the best part of every dish she cooks.

[115]

§ 51

That George Bernard Shaw doesn't really believe anything he writes.

§ 52

That the music of Richard Wagner is all played *fortissimo*, and by cornets.

§ 53

That the Masonic order goes back to the days of King Solomon.

§ 54

That swearing is forbidden by the Bible.

§ 55

That all newspaper reporters carry notebooks.

§ 56

That whiskey is good for snake-bite.

§ 57

That surgeons often kill patients for the sheer pleasure of it.

§ 58

That ten drops of camphor in half a glass of water will prevent a cold.

[116]

§ 59

That the first thing a country jake does when he comes to New York is to make a bee line for Grant's Tomb and the Aquarium.

§ 60

That if one's nose tickles it is a sign that one is going to meet a stranger or kiss a fool.

§ 61

That if one's right ear burns, it is a sign that some one is saying nice things about one.

§ 62

That if one's left ear burns, it is a sign that some one is saying mean things about one.

§ 63

That French women use great quantities of perfume in lieu of taking a bath.

§ 64

That a six-footer is invariably a virtuoso of amour superior to a man of, say, five feet seven.

[117]

§ 65

That a soubrette is always fifteen or twenty years older than she looks.

§ 66

That what impels most men to have their finger-nails manicured is a vanity for having manicured finger-nails.

§ 67

That water rots the hair and thus causes baldness.

§ 68

That when one twin dies, the other twin becomes exceedingly melancholy and soon also dies.

§ 69

That one may always successfully get a cinder out of the eye by not touching the eye, but by rolling it in an outward direction and simultaneously blowing the nose.

§ 70

That if one wears light weight underwear winter and summer the year 'round, one will never catch a cold.

§ 71

That a drunken man is invariably more bellicose than a sober man.

§ 72

That all prize-fighters and baseball players have their hair cut round in the back.

§ 73

That the work of a detective calls for exceptionally high sagacity and cunning.

§ 74

That on the first day of the season in the pleasure parks many persons, owing to insufficiently tested apparatus, are regularly killed on the roller-coasters.

§ 75

That a play, a novel, or a short story with a happy ending is necessarily a commercialized and inartistic piece of work.

§ 76

That a person who follows up a cucumber salad

with a dish of ice-cream will inevitably be the victim of cholera morbus.

§ 77

That a Sunday School superintendent is always carrying on an intrigue with one of the girls in the choir.

§ 78

That it is one of the marks of a gentleman that he never speaks evil of a woman.

§ 79

That a member of the Masons cannot be hanged.

§ 80

That a policeman can eat *gratis* as much fruit and as many peanuts off the street-corner stands as he wants.

§ 81

That the real President of the United States is J. P. Morgan.

§ 82

That onion breath may be promptly removed by drinking a little milk.

§ 83

That onion breath may be promptly removed by eating a little parsley.

§ 84

That Catholic priests conduct their private conversations in Latin.

§ 85

That John Drew is a great society man.

§ 86

That all Swedes are stupid fellows, and have very thick skulls.

§ 87

That all the posthumously printed stories of David Graham Phillips and Jack London have been written by hacks hired by the magazine editors and publishers.

§ 88

That a man like Charles Schwab, who has made a great success of the steel business, could in the same way easily have become a great composer like Bach or Mozart had he been minded thus to devote his talents.

§ 89

That the man who doesn't hop promptly to his feet when the orchestra plays "The Star Spangled Banner" as an overture to Hurtig and Seamon's "Hurly-Burly Girlies" must have either rheumatism or pro-Bolshevik sympathies.

§ 90

That every workman in Henry Ford's factory owns a pretty house in the suburbs and has a rose-garden in the back-yard.

§ 91

That all circus people are very pure and lead domestic lives.

§ 92

That if a spark hits a celluloid collar, the collar will explode.

§ 93

That when a bachelor who has hated children for twenty years gets married and discovers he is about to become a father, he is delighted.

[122]

§ 94

That drinking three drinks of whiskey a day will prevent pneumonia.

§ 95

That every negro who went to France with the army had a liaison with a white woman and won't look at a nigger wench any more.

§ 96

That all Russians have unpronounceable names.

§ 97

That awnings keep rooms cool.

§ 98

That it is very difficult to decipher a railroad time-table.

§ 99

That gamblers may always be identified by their habit of wearing large diamonds.

§ 100

That when a man embarks in a canoe with a girl,

[123]

the chances are two to one that the girl will move around when the boat is in mid-stream and upset it.

§ 101

That German babies are brought up on beer in place of milk.

§ 102

That a man with two shots of cocaine in him could lick Jack Dempsey.

§ 103

That fully one half the repertoire of physical ailments is due to uric acid.

§ 104

That a woman, when buying a cravat for a man, always picks out one of green and purple with red polka-dots.

§ 105

That a negro's vote may always be readily bought for a dollar.

§ 106

That cripples always have very sunny dispositions.

[124]

§ 107

That if one drops a crust of bread into one's glass of champagne, one can drink indefinitely without getting drunk.

§ 108

That a brass band always makes one feel like marching.

§ 109

That, when shaving on a railway train, a man invariably cuts himself.

§ 110

That the male Spaniard is generally a handsome, flashing-eyed fellow, possessed of fiery temper.

§ 111

That after drinking a glass of absinthe one has peculiar hallucinations and nightmares.

§ 112

That since the Indians were never bald, baldness comes from wearing tight hats.

[125]

§ 113

That all wine-agents are very loose men.

§ 114

That the editor of a woman's magazine is always a lizzie.

§ 115

That what is contained in the pitcher on the speakers' platform is always ice-water.

§ 116

That all Senators from Texas wear sombreros, chew tobacco, expectorate profusely, and frequently employ the word "maverick."

§ 117

That the meters on taxicabs are covertly manipulated by the chauffeurs by means of wires hidden under the latters' seats.

§ 118

That Lillian Russell is as beautiful today as she was thirty-five years ago.

[126]

§ 119

That if a young woman can hold a lighted match in her fingers until it completely burns up, it is a sign that her young man really loves her.

§ 120

That if a young woman accidentally puts on her lingerie wrong side out, it is a sign that she will be married before the end of the year.

§ 121

That if a bride wears an old garter with her new finery, she will have a happy married life.

§ 122

That a sudden chill is a sign that somebody is walking over one's grave.

§ 123

That some ignoble Italian is at the bottom of every Dorothy Arnold *fugax.*

§ 124

That a tarantula will not crawl over a piece of rope.

[127]

§ 125

That millionaires always go to sleep at the opera.

§ 126

That Paderewski can get all the pianos he wants for nothing.

§ 127

That a bloodhound never makes a mistake.

§ 128

That celery is good for the nerves.

§ 129

That the jokes in *Punch* are never funny.

§ 130

That the Mohammedans are heathens.

§ 131

That a sudden shock may cause the hair to turn grey over night.

§ 132

That the farmer is an honest man, and greatly imposed upon.

[128]

§ 133

That all the antique furniture sold in America is made in Grand Rapids, Mich., and that the holes testifying to its age are made either with gimlets or by trained worms.

§ 134

That if a dog is fond of a man it is an infallible sign that the man is a good sort, and one to be trusted.

§ 135

That blondes are flightier than brunettes.

§ 136

That a nurse, however ugly, always looks beautiful to the sick man.

§ 137

That book-keepers are always round-shouldered.

§ 138

That if one touches a hop-toad, one will get warts.

§ 139

That a collar-button that drops to the floor when

[129]

one is dressing invariably rolls into an obscure and inaccessible spot and eludes the explorations of its owner.

§ 140

That an American ambassador has the French, German, Italian, Spanish, Portuguese, Russian and Japanese languages at his finger tips, and is chummy with royalty.

§ 141

That the ready-made mail order blue serge suits for men are put together with mucilage, and turn green after they have been in the sunlight for a day or two.

§ 142

That if one has only three matches left, the first two will invariably go out, but that the third and last will remain lighted.

§ 143

That all Chinamen smoke opium.

§ 144

That every country girl who falls has been seduced by a man from the city.

[130]

§ 145

That an intelligent prize-fighter always triumphs over an ignorant prize-fighter, however superior the latter in agility and strength.

§ 146

That a doctor's family never gets sick.

§ 147

That nature designed a horse's tail primarily as a flicker-off of flies.

§ 148

That nicotine keeps the teeth in a sound condition.

§ 149

That when an Odd Fellow dies he is always given a magnificent funeral by his lodge, including a band and a parade.

§ 150

That the man who is elected president of the Senior Class in a college is always the most popular man in his class.

§ 151

That a minor actress in a theatrical company always considers the leading man a superb creature, and loves him at a distance.

§ 152

That a Southern levee is a gay place.

§ 153

That when a dog whines in the middle of the night, it is a sure sign that some one is going to die.

§ 154

That the stenographer in a business house is always coveted by her employer, who invites her to luncheon frequently, gradually worms his way into her confidence, keeps her after office hours one day, accomplishes her ruin, and then sets her up in a magnificently furnished apartment in Riverside Drive and appeases her old mother by paying the latter's expenses for a summer holiday with her daughter at the seashore.

§ 155

That the extinction of the Indian has been a deplorable thing.

§ 156

That everybody has a stomach-ache after Thanksgiving dinner.

§ 157

That, in summer, tan shoes are much cooler on the feet than black shoes.

§ 158

That every man who calls himself Redmond is a Jew whose real name is Rosenberg.

§ 159

That General Grant never directed a battle save with a cigar in his mouth.

§ 160

That there is something slightly peculiar about a man who wears spats.

§ 161

That the more modest a young girl is, the more innocent she is.

§ 162

That what a woman admires above everything else in a man is an upright character.

[133]

§ 163

That seafaring men drink nothing but rum.

§ 164

That no family in the slums has less than six children.

§ 165

That a piece of camphor worn on a string around the neck will ward off disease.

§ 166

That a saloon with a sign reading "Family Entrance" on its side door invariably has a bawdy house upstairs.

§ 167

That the wife of a rich man always wistfully looks back into the past and wishes she had married a poor man.

§ 168

That all persons prominent in smart society are very dull.

§ 169

That when ordering a drink of whiskey at a bar,

a man always used to instruct the bartender as to the size of the drink he desired by saying "two fingers" or "three fingers."

§ 170

That all the wine formerly served in Italian restaurants was made in the cellar, and was artificially coloured with some sort of dye that was very harmful to the stomach.

§ 171

That all criminals get caught sooner or later.

§ 172

That stokers on ocean liners are from long service so used to the heat of the furnaces that they don't notice it.

§ 173

That what draws men to horse races is love of the sport.

§ 174

That tarantulas often come from the tropics in bunches of bananas, and that when one of them

[135]

stings a negro on the wharf he swells up, turns green and dies within three hours.

§ 175

That a man will do anything for the woman he loves.

§ 176

That the reason William Gillette, who has been acting for over forty years, always smokes cigars in the parts he plays is because he is very nervous when on the stage.

§ 177

That the doughnut is an exceptionally indigest-. ible article.

§ 178

That one captive balloon in every two containing persons on pleasure bent breaks away from its moorings, and drifts out to sea.

§ 179

That a workingman always eats what is in his dinnerpail with great relish.

[136]

§ 180

That children were much better behaved twenty years ago than they are today.

§ 181

That the cashier of a restaurant in adding up a customer's cheque always adds a dollar which is subsequently split between himself and the waiter.

§ 182

That it is impossible to pronounce the word "statistics" without stuttering.

§ 183

That the profession of white slaving, in 1900 controlled exclusively by Chinamen, has since passed entirely under the control of Italians.

§ 184

That every person in the Riviera lives in a "villa."

§ 185

That the chief form of headgear among the Swiss is the Alpine hat.

[137]

§ 186

That each year a man volunteers to take his children to the circus merely as a subterfuge to go himself.

§ 187

That all marriages with actresses turn out badly.

§ 188

That San Francisco is a very gay place, and full of opium joints.

§ 189

That an elevator operator never succeeds in stopping his car on a level with the floor.

§ 190

That they don't make any pianos today as good as the old square ones.

§ 191

That a man who habitually clears his throat before he speaks is generally a self-important hypocrite and a bluffer.

[138]

§ 192

That Maurice Maeterlinck, the Belgian Dr. Frank Crane, leads a monastic life.

§ 193

That whenever a vaudeville comedian quotes a familiar commercial slogan, such as "His Master's Voice," or "Eventually, why not now?", he is paid $50 a performance for doing so.

§ 194

That all Asiatic idols have large precious rubies in their foreheads.

§ 195

That when the foe beheld Joan of Arc leading the French army against them, a look of terror froze their features and that, casting their arms from them, they broke into a frenzied and precipitate flight.

§ 196

That the late King Edward VII as Prince of Wales easily got every girl he wanted.

[139]

§ 197

That the penitentiaries of the United States contain a great number of hapless prisoners possessed of a genuine gift for poetry.

§ 198

That if a cat gets into a room where a baby is sleeping, the cat will suck the baby's breath and kill it.

§ 199

That all men named Clarence, Claude or Percy are sissies.

§ 200

That a street car conductor steals every fifth nickel.

§ 201

That the security of a bank is to be estimated in proportion to the solidity of the bank building.

§ 202

That seventy-five per cent of all taxicab drivers have at one time or another been in Sing Sing.

§ 203

That one can buy a fine suit of clothes in London for twelve dollars.

§ 204

That the chicken salad served in restaurants is always made of veal.

§ 205

That a play without a bed in it never makes any money in Paris.

§ 206

That Conan Doyle would have made a wonderful detective.

§ 207

That an oyster-shucker every month or so discovers a pearl which he goes out and sells for five hundred dollars.

§ 208

That a napkin is always wrapped around a champagne bottle for the purpose of hiding the label, and that the quality of the champagne may be judged by the amount of noise the cork makes when it is popped.

[141]

§ 209

That because a married woman remains loyal to her husband she loves him.

§ 210

That every time one blows oneself to a particularly expensive cigar and leans back to enjoy oneself with a good smoke after a hearty and satisfying dinner, the cigar proceeds to burn down the side.

§ 211

That when a police captain goes on a holiday he always gets boilingly drunk.

§ 212

That an Italian puts garlic in everything he eats, including coffee.

§ 213

That if one hits a negro on the head with a cobblestone, the cobblestone will break.

§ 214

That all nuns have entered convents because of unfortunate love affairs.

§ 215

That, being surrounded by alcoholic beverages and believing the temptation would be irresistible once he began, a bartender in the old days never took a drink.

§ 216

That all millionaires are born in small ram-shackle houses situated near railroad tracks.

§ 217

That farmers afford particularly easy prey for book-agents and are the largest purchasers of cheap sets of Guy de Maupassant, Rudyard Kipling and O. Henry.

§ 218

That George Washington never told a lie.

§ 219

That a dark cigar is always a strong one.

§ 220

That the night air is poisonous.

[143]

§ 221

That a hair from a horse's tail, if put into a bottle of water, will turn into a snake.

§ 222

That champagne is the best of all wines.

§ 223

That it snowed every Christmas down to fifteen years ago.

§ 224

That if a young woman finds a piece of tea leaf floating around the top of her tea cup, it is a sign that she will be married before the end of the year.

§ 225

That if, after one lusty blow, a girl's birthday cake reveals nine candles still burning, it is a sign that it will be nine years before she gets married.

§ 226

That if, while promenading, a girl and her escort walk on either side of a water hydrant or other obstruction instead of both walking 'round it

[144]

on the same side, they will have a misunderstanding before the month is over.

§ 227

That it is unlikely that a man and woman who enter a hotel without baggage after 10 P. M. and register are man and wife.

§ 228

That all country girls have clear, fresh, rosy complexions.

§ 229

That chorus girls spend the time during the entr'-actes sitting around naked in their dressing-rooms telling naughty stories.

§ 230

That many soldiers' lives have been saved in battle by bullets lodging in Bibles which they have carried in their breast pockets.

§ 231

That each year the Fourth of July exodus to the bathing beaches on the part of persons from the city establishes a new record.

§ 232

That women with red hair or wide nostrils are possessed of especially passionate natures.

§ 233

That three-fourths of the inhabitants of Denver are lungers who have gone there for the mountain air.

§ 234

That, when sojourning in Italy, one always feels very lazy.

§ 235

That the people of Johnstown, Pa., still talk of nothing but the flood.

§ 236

That there is no finer smell in the world than that of burning autumn leaves.

§ 237

That Jules Verne anticipated all the great modern inventions.

§ 238

That a man is always a much heartier eater than a woman.

[146]

§ 239

That all the girls in Mr. Ziegfeld's "Follies" are extraordinarily seductive, and that at least 40 head of bank cashiers are annually guilty of tapping the till ·in order to buy them diamonds and Russian sables.

§ 240

That a college sophomore is always a complete ignoramus.

§ 241

That rubbers in wet weather are a preventive of colds.

§ 242

That if one eats oysters in a month not containing an "r," one is certain to get ptomaine poisoning.

§ 243

That a woman with a 7½-C foot always tries to squeeze it into a 4½-A shoe.

§ 244

That no shop girl ever reads anything but Laura Jean Libbey and the cheap sex magazines.

§ 245

That there is something peculiar about a man who wears a red tie.

§ 246

That all Bolsheviki and Anarchists have whiskers.

§ 247

That all the millionaires of Pittsburgh are very loud fellows, and raise merry hell with the chorus girls every time they go to New York.

§ 248

That a man of fifty-five is always more experienced than a man of thirty-five.

§ 249

That new Bermuda potatoes come from Bermuda.

§ 250

That the boy who regularly stands at the foot of his class in school always turns out in later life to be very successful.

§ 251

That the ornamental daggers fashioned out of one hundred dollars' worth of Chinese coins strung together, which one buys in Pekin or Hong Kong for three dollars and a quarter, are fashioned out of one hundred dollars' worth of Chinese coins.

§ 252

That it is hard to find any one in Hoboken, N. J., who can speak English.

§ 253

That the headwaiter in a fashionable restaurant has better manners than any other man in the place.

§ 254

That a girl always likes best the man who is possessed of a cavalier politeness.

§ 255

That the most comfortable room conceivable is one containing a great big open fireplace.

§ 256

That brunettes are more likely to grow stout in later years than blondes.

§ 257

That a sepia photograph of the Coliseum, framed, is a work of art.

§ 258

That every time one crosses the English Channel one encounters rough weather and is very sea-sick.

§ 259

That the Navajo blankets sold to trans-continental tourists by the Indians on the station platform at Albuquerque, New Mexico, are made by the Elite Novelty M'f'g. Co. of Passaic, N. J., and are bought by the Indians in lots of 1,000.

§ 260

That appendicitis is an ailment invented by surgeons twelve years ago for money-making purposes and that, in the century before that time, no one was ever troubled with it.

[150]

§ 261

That a theatrical matinée performance is always inferior to an evening performance, the star being always eager to hurry up the show in order to get a longer period for rest before the night performance.

§ 262

That John D. Rockefeller would give his whole fortune for a digestion good enough to digest a cruller.

§ 263

That a clergyman leads an easy and lazy life, and spends most of his time visiting women parishioners while their husbands are at work.

§ 264

That it is almost sure death to eat cucumbers and drink milk at the same meal.

§ 265

That all bank cashiers, soon or late, tap the till.

§ 266

That the members of fashionable church choirs,

[151]

during the sermon, engage in kissing and hugging behind the pipe-organ.

§ 267

That women who are in society never pay any attention to their children, and wish that they would die.

§ 268

That if one gets one's feet wet, one is sure to catch cold.

§ 269

That all French women are very passionate, and will sacrifice everything to love.

§ 270

That when a drunken man falls he never hurts himself.

§ 271

That all Chinese laundrymen sprinkle their laundry by taking a mouthful of water and squirting it out at their wash in a fine spray; and that, whatever the cost of living to a white man, the Chinese laundryman always lives on eight cents a day.

§ 272

That if one fixes a savage beast with one's eye, the beast will remain rooted to the spot and presently slink away.

§ 273

That if one eats cucumbers and then goes in swimming, one will be seized with a cramp.

§ 274

That hiccoughs may be stopped by counting slowly up to one hundred.

§ 275

That newspaper reporters hear, every day, a great many thumping scandals that they fail to print, and that they refrain through considerations of honour.

§ 276

That the young East Side fellow who plays violin solos at the moving-picture theatre around the corner is so talented that, if he had the money to go to Europe to study, he would be a rival to Kreisler within three years.

§ 277

· That Paderewski, during the piano-playing days, wore a wig, and was actually as bald as a coot.

§ 278

That lightning never strikes twice in the same place.

§ 279

That when a doctor finds there is nothing the matter with a man who has come to consult him, he never frankly tells the man there's nothing wrong with him, but always gives him bread pills.

§ 280

That, in a family crisis, the son always sticks to the mother and the daughter to the father.

§ 281

That beer is very fattening.

§ 282

That no man of first-rate mental attainments ever goes in for dancing.

[154]

§ 283

That a woman can't sharpen a lead pencil.

§ 284

That on every trans-Atlantic steamer there are two smooth gamblers who, the moment the ship docks, sneak over the side with the large sum of money they have won from the passengers.

§ 285

That if one gets out of bed on the left side in the morning, one has a mean disposition for the rest of the day.

§ 286

That a woman who has led a loose life is so grateful for the respect shown her by the man who asks her to marry him that she makes the best kind of wife.

§ 287

That fish is a brain food.

§ 288

That street-corner beggars have a great deal of

money hidden away at home under the kitchen floor.

§ 289

That it is advisable for a young woman who takes gas when having a tooth pulled to be accompanied by some one, by way of precaution against the dentist.

§ 290

That all girls educated in convents turn out in later life to be hell-raisers.

§ 291

That a young girl may always safely be trusted with the kind of man who speaks of his mother.

§ 292

That a nine-year-old boy who likes to play with toy steam engines is probably a born mechanical genius and should be educated to be an engineer.

§ 293

That all celebrated professional humourists are in private life heavy and witless fellows.

§ 294

That when one stands close to the edge of a dizzy altitude, one is seized peculiarly with an impulse to jump off.

§ 295

That if one eats an apple every night before retiring, one will never be ill.

§ 296

That all negroes born south of the Potomac can play the banjo and are excellent dancers.

§ 297

That whenever a negro is educated he refuses to work and becomes a criminal.

§ 298

That whenever an Italian begins to dress like an American and to drive a Dodge car, it is a sign he has taken to black-handing or has acquired an interest in the white-slave trust.

§ 299

That, in the days when there were breweries, the men who drove beer-wagons drank 65 glasses of beer a head a day, and that it didn't hurt them because it came direct from the wood.

§ 300

That, until the time of American intervention, the people of the Philippines were all cannibals, and displayed the heads of their fallen enemies on poles in front of their houses.

§ 301

That whenever a crowd of boys goes camping in summer two or three of them are drowned, and the rest come home suffering from poison ivy.

§ 302

That whenever a will case gets into the courts, the lawyers gobble all the money, and the heirs come out penniless.

§ 303

That every female moving-picture star carries on an intrigue with her leading man, and will marry him as soon as he can get rid of his poor first wife, who took in washing in order to pay for his education in the art of acting.

[158]

§ 304

That all theatrical managers are Jews, and that most of them can scarcely speak English.

§ 305

That a great many of women's serious diseases are due to high French heels.

§ 306

That if one does not scratch a mosquito bite, it will stop itching.

§ 307

That when a girl gives a man a pen-knife for a present, their friendship will come to an unhappy end unless he exercises the precaution to ward off bad luck by giving her a penny.

§ 308

That whenever one takes an umbrella with one, it doesn't rain.

§ 309

That the cloth used in suits made in England is so good that it never wears out.

§ 310

That cinnamon drops are coloured red with a dye-stuff manufactured out of the dried bodies of cochineal insects.

§ 311

That the missionaries in China and Africa make fortunes robbing the natives they are sent out to convert.

§ 312

That there is a revolution in Central America every morning before breakfast, and that the sole object of all the revolutionary chiefs is to seize the money in the public treasury and make off to Paris.

§ 313

That whenever there is a funeral in an Irish family the mourners all get drunk and proceed to assault one another with clubs.

§ 314

That all immigrants come to America in search of liberty, and that when they attempt to exercise it they should be immediately sent back.

[160]

§ 315

That whenever a rich American girl marries a foreign nobleman, he at once gets hold of all her money, then beats her and then runs away with an actress.

§ 316

That if one begins eating peanuts one cannot stop.

§ 317

That a bachelor never has any one to sew the buttons on his clothes.

§ 318

That whenever a dog wags his tail it is a sign that he is particularly happy.

§ 319

That an Italian street labourer can do a hard day's work on one large plate of spaghetti a day.

§ 320

That if one breaks a mirror one will have bad luck for seven years.

[161]

§ 321

That two men seldom agree that the same girl is good-looking.

§ 322

That in the infinitesimal space of time between the springing of the trap-door and his dropping through it, a hanged man sees his entire life pass in panorama before him.

§ 323

That when Washington crossed the Delaware, he stood up in the bow of the boat holding aloft a large American flag.

§ 324

That whereas a man always hopes his first child will be a boy, his wife always hopes that it will be a girl.

§ 325

That the first time a boy smokes a cigar he always becomes deathly sick.

§ 326

That a woman always makes a practice of being

[162]

deliberately late in keeping an appointment with a man.

§ 327

That if, encountering a savage beast in the jungle, one falls upon the ground, lies still and pretends that one is dead, the savage beast will promptly make off and not hurt one.

§ 328

That if one sits in front of the Café de la Paix, in Paris, one will soon or late see everybody in the world that one knows.

§ 329

That it is always twice as hard to get rid of a summer cold as to get rid of a winter cold.

§ 330

That a soft speaking voice is the invariable mark of a well-bred man.

§ 331

That the persons who most vociferously applaud the playing of "Dixie" in restaurants are all North-

erners who have never been further South than
Allentown, Pa.

§ 332

That the larger the dog, the safer he is for children.

§ 333

That Catholic priests never solicit money from
their parishioners, but merely assess them so much
a head, and make them pay up instantly.

§ 334

That nine times in ten when one is in pain, and
a doctor assures one that he is squirting morphine
into one's arm, what he is really squirting in is
only warm water.

§ 335

That a German civilian, before the war, had to
get off the sidewalk whenever an army lieutenant
approached him on the street, and that, if he failed
to do so instantly, the lieutenant was free to run
him through with his sword.

§ 336

That while it may be possible, in every individual case of spiritualist communication with the dead, to prove fraud by the medium, the accumulated effect of such communications is to demonstrate the immortality of the soul.

§ 337

That an Italian who earns and saves $1,000 in America can take the money home, invest it in an estate, and live like a rich man thereafter.

§ 338

That all Mormons, despite the laws against it, still practise polygamy, and that they have agents all over the world recruiting cuties for their harems.

§ 339

That when a man goes to a photographer's to have his picture taken, the knowledge that he is having his picture taken always makes him very self-conscious, thus causing him to assume an expression which results in the photograph being an inaccurate likeness.

§ 340

That if the lower line on the palm of one's hand

[165]

is a long one, it is a sign that one is going to live to a ripe old age.

§ 341

That Italian counts, before the war, always used to make their expenses when they came to America by acting as wine agents.

§ 342

That a Russian peasant, in the days of the czar, drank two quarts of vodka a day.

§ 343

That a German farmer can raise more produce on one acre of land than an American can raise on a hundred.

§ 344

That a boil on the neck purifies the blood and is worth $1,000.

§ 345

That whenever a Frenchman comes home unexpectedly, some friend of the family makes a quick sneak out of the back door.

§ 346

That every negro servant girl spends at least half of her wages on preparations for taking the kink out of her hair.

§ 347

That the licorice candy sold in cheap candy stores is made of old rubber boots.

§ 348

That if a boy is given all he wants to drink at home he will not drink when he is away from home.

§ 349

That the second-class passengers on a trans-Atlantic steamship always have more fun than the first-class passengers.

§ 350

That a drunken man always pronounces every "s" as "sh."

§ 351

That champagne will prevent seasickness.

[167]

§ 352

That thin wrists and slender ankles are unmistakable signs of aristocratic breeding.

§ 353

That when one asks a girl to go canoeing she always brings along a bright red or yellow sofa cushion.

§ 354

That when a woman buys cigars for a man she always judges the quality of the cigars by the magnificence of the cigar-bands.

§ 355

That candle light makes a woman forty-five years old look fifteen years younger.

§ 356

That the winters in the United States are a good deal less cold than they used to be, and that the change has been caused by the Gulf Stream.

§ 357

That the Thursday matinées given by Chauncey Olcott are attended only by Irish servant girls.

[168]

§ 358

That the reason the British authorities didn't lock up Bernard Shaw during the war was because they were afraid of his mind.

§ 359

That Professor Garner was able to carry on long and intimate conversations with monkeys in their own language.

§ 360

That oysters are a great aphrodisiac.

§ 361

That if one sleeps with one's head on a high pillow one will be round-shouldered.

§ 362

That coal miners get so dirty that they have to wash so often that they are the cleanest working-men in the world.

§ 363

That the average French housewife can make such a soup out of the contents of a garbage-can that the eater will think he is at the Ritz.

§ 364

That such authors as Dr. Frank Crane and Herbert Kaufman do not really believe what they write, but print it simply for the money that is in it.

§ 365

That the average newspaper cartoonist makes $100,000 a year.

§ 366

That when a play is given in an insane asylum the inmates always laugh at the tragic moments and cry at the humorous moments.

§ 367

That if a girl takes the last cake off a plate she will die an old maid.

§ 368

That men high in public affairs always read detective stories for diversion.

§ 369

That the wireless news bulletins posted daily on ocean liners are made up on board.

§ 370

That the Swiss, when they sing, always yodel.

§ 371

That all German housewives are very frugal.

§ 372

That if one holds a buttercup under a person's chin and a yellow light is reflected upon that person's chin, it is a sign that he likes butter.

§ 373

That all penny-in-the-slot weighing machines make a fat woman lighter and a thin woman heavier.

§ 374

That in the period just before a woman's baby is born the woman's face takes on a peculiar spiritual and holy look.

§ 375

That when a Chinese laundryman hands one a slip for one's laundry, the Chinese letters which he writes on the slip have nothing to do with the

[171]

laundry but are in reality a derogatory description of the owner.

§ 376

That an old woman with rheumatism in her leg can infallibly predict when it is going to rain.

§ 377

That Philadelphia is a very sleepy town.

§ 378

That it is impossible for a man to learn how to thread a needle.

§ 379

That there is something unmanly about a grown man playing the piano, save only when he plays it in a bordello.

§ 380

That a couple of quinine pills, with a chaser of rye whiskey, will cure a cold.

§ 381

That all Congressmen who voted for Prohibition are secret lushers and have heavy stocks of all sorts of liquors in their cellars.

§ 382

That a recent President of the United States was a great fellow with the gals, and used to carry on with a stock-company actress.

§ 383

That all the best cooks are men.

§ 384

That all Japanese butlers are lieutenants in the Japanese Navy and that they read and copy all letters received by the folks they work for.

§ 385

That the best way to stop nose-bleed is to drop a door-key down the patient's back.

§ 386

That a thunder-storm will cause milk to turn sour.

§ 387

That if a man drinks three glasses of buttermilk every day he will never be ill.

[173]

§ 388

That whenever two Indians meet they greet each other with the word "How!"

§ 389

That the Justices of the Supreme Court of the United States all chew tobacco while hearing cases, but that they are very serious men otherwise, and never laugh, or look at a pretty girl, or get tight.

§ 390

That all negro prize-fighters marry white women, and that they afterward beat them.

§ 391

That New Orleans is a very gay town and full of beautiful French creoles.

§ 392

That gin is good for the kidneys.

§ 393

That the English lower classes are so servile that they say "Thank you, sir," if one kicks them in the pantaloons.

[174]

§ 394

That the gipsies who go about the country are all horse-thieves, and that they will put a spell upon the cattle of any farmer who has them arrested for stealing his mare.

§ 395

That every bachelor of easy means has an illicit affair with a grass widow in a near-by city and is the father of several illegitimate children.

§ 396

That a country editor receives so many presents of potatoes, corn, rutabagas, asparagus, country ham, carrots, turnips, etc., that he never has to buy any food.

§ 397

That whenever news reached him of another Federal disaster Abraham Lincoln would laugh it off with a very funny and often somewhat smutty story, made up on the spot.

§ 398

That George Washington died of a heavy cold brought on by swimming the Potomac in the heart

[175]

of winter to visit a yellow girl on the Maryland shore.

§ 399

That all negroes who show any intelligence whatever are actually two-thirds white, and the sons of United States Senators.

§ 400

That the late King Leopold of Belgium left 350 illegitimate children.

§ 401

That Senator Henry Cabot Lodge is a very brainy man, though somewhat stuck up.

§ 402

That if one eats ice-cream after lobster one will be doubled up by belly-ache.

§ 403

That Quakers, for all their religion, are always very sharp traders and have a great deal of money hidden away in banks.

[176]

§ 404

That old baseball players always take to booze, and so end their days either as panhandlers, as night watchmen or as janitors of Odd Fellows' halls.

§ 405

That the object of the players, in college football, is to gouge out one another's eyes and pull off one another's ears.

§ 406

That the sort of woman who carries around a Pomeranian dog, if she should ever have a child inadvertently, would give the midwife $500 to make away with it.

§ 407

That a woman likes to go to a bargain sale, fight her way to the counter, and have pins stuck into her and her feet mashed by other women.

§ 408

That, if one swallows an ounce of olive oil before going to a banquet, one will not get drunk.

[177]

§ 409

That a mud-turtle is so tenacious of life that if one cuts off his head a new one will grow in its place.

§ 410

That the only things farmers read are government documents and patent-medicine almanacs.

§ 411

That if one's ear itches it is a sign that some one is talking of one.

§ 412

That Italian children, immediately they leave the cradle, are sewed into their underclothes, and that they never get a bath thereafter until they are confirmed.

§ 413

That all Catholic priests are very hearty eaters, and have good wine cellars.

§ 414

That politics in America would be improved by turning all the public offices over to business men.

[178]

§ 415

That department store sales are always fakes, and that they mark down a few things to attract the women and then swindle them by lifting the prices on things they actually want.

§ 416

That 100,000 abortions are performed in Chicago every year.

§ 417

That John D. Rockefeller has a great mind, and would make a fine President if it were not for his craze for money.

§ 418

That all the Jews who were drafted during the late war were put into the Quartermaster's Department on account of their extraordinary business acumen.

§ 419

That a jury never convicts a pretty woman.

§ 420

That chorus girls in the old days got so tired of

drinking champagne that the sound of a cork popping made them shudder.

§ 421

That the Massachusetts troops, after the first battle of Bull Run, didn't stop running until they reached Harrisburg, Pa.

§ 422

That General Grant was always soused during a battle, and that on the few occasions when he was sober he got licked.

§ 423

That the late King Edward used to carry on in Paris at such a gait that he shocked even the Parisians.

§ 424

That it takes an Englishman two days to see a joke, and that he always gets it backward even then.

§ 425

That headwaiters in fashionable hotels make $100 a day.

§ 426

That if a bat flies into a woman's hair, the hair must be cut off to get it out.

§ 427

That all the women in Chicago have very large feet.

§ 428

That on cold nights policemen always sneak into stables on their beats and go to sleep.

§ 429

That all the schoolboys in Boston have bulged brows, wear large spectacles and can read Greek.

§ 430

That all dachshunds come from Germany.

§ 431

That nine out of every ten Frenchmen have syphilis.

§ 432

That the frankfurters sold at circuses and pleasure parks are made of dog meat.

[181]

§ 433

That all the cheaper brands of cigarettes are sophisticated with drugs, and in time cause those who smoke them to get softening of the brain.

§ 434

That rock-and-rye will cure a cold.

§ 435

That a country boy armed with a bent pin can catch more fish than a city angler with the latest and most expensive tackle.

§ 436

That red-haired girls are especially virulent.

§ 437

That all gamblers eventually go broke.

§ 438

That the worst actress in the company is always the manager's wife.

§ 439

That an elephant in a circus never forgets a person who gives him a chew of tobacco or a rotten peanut, but will single him out from a crowd years afterward and bash in his head with one colossal blow.

§ 440

That it is unlucky to put your hat on a bed.

§ 441

That an old sock makes the best wrapping for a sore throat.

§ 442

That lighting three cigarettes with one match will bring some terrible calamity upon one or other of the three smokers.

§ 443

That milking a cow is an operation demanding a special talent that is possessed only by yokels, and that a person born in a large city can never hope to acquire it.

§ 444

That whenever there is a rough-house during a strike, it is caused by foreign anarchists who are trying to knock out American idealism.

[183]

§ 445

That, whatever the demerits of Jews otherwise, they are always very kind to their old parents.

§ 446

That the Swiss army, though small, is so strong that not even the German army in its palmy days could have invaded Switzerland, and that it is strong because all Swiss are patriots to the death.

§ 447

That when two Frenchmen fight a duel, whether with pistols or with swords, neither of them is ever hurt half so much as he would have been had he fought an honest American wearing boxing-gloves.

§ 448

That whenever Prohibition is enforced in a region populated by negroes, they take to morphine, heroin and other powerful drugs, and begin murdering all of the white inhabitants.

§ 449

That all the great writers of the world now use typewriters.

§ 450

That all Presidents of the United States get many hot tips on the stock-market, but that they are too honourable to play them, and so turn them over to their wives, who make fortunes out of them.

§ 451

That Elihu Root is an intellectual giant, and that it is a pity the suspicion of him among farmers makes it impossible to elect him President.

§ 452

That no man not a sissy can ever learn to thread a needle or darn a sock.

§ 453

That all glass blowers soon or late die of consumption.

§ 454

That all women who go in bathing at the French seaside resorts affect very naughty one-piece bathing suits.

§ 455

That George M. Cohan and Irving Berlin can only play the piano with one finger.

§ 456

That farmers always go into gold mine swindles because of the magnificently embossed stock certificates.

§ 457

That the Germans eat six regular meals a day, and between times stave off their appetite with numerous Schweitzer cheese sandwiches, blutwurst and beer.

§ 458

That David Belasco teaches his actresses how to express emotion by knocking them down and pulling them around the stage by the hair.

§ 459

That only Americans travel in the first class carriages of foreign railway trains, and that fashionable Englishmen always travel third class.

§ 460

That the whiskey sold in blind pigs contains wood alcohol and causes those who drink it to go blind.

§ 461

That wealthy society women never wear their pearl necklaces in public, but always keep them at home in safes and wear indistinguishable imitations instead.

§ 462

That the late Charles Yerkes had no less than twenty girls, for each of whom he provided a Fifth Avenue mansion and a yearly income of $50,000.

§ 463

That when one goes to a railroad station to meet some one, the train is never on time.

§ 464

That the theatregoers in the Scandinavian countries care for nothing but Ibsen and Strindberg.

§ 465

That all doctors write prescriptions illegibly.

§ 466

That Englishwomen are very cold.

§ 467

That when the weather man predicts rain it always turns out fair, and that when he predicts fair it always rains.

§ 468

That lemon juice will remove freckles.

§ 469

That if a woman wears a string of amber beads she will never get a sore throat.

§ 470

That no well-bred person ever chews gum.

§ 471

That all actors sleep till noon, and spend the afternoon calling on women.

§ 472

That the men who make sauerkraut press it into barrels by jumping on it with their bare feet.

§ 473

That the moment a nigger gets eight dollars, he goes to a dentist and has one of his front teeth filled with gold.

§ 474

That one never sees a Frenchman drunk, all the souses whom one sees in Paris being Americans.

§ 475

That a daughter is always a much greater comfort to a mother in after life than a son.

§ 476

That a man with a weak, receding chin is always a nincompoop.

§ 477

That English butlers always look down on their American employers, and frequently have to leave the room to keep from laughing out loud.

§ 478

That the most faithful and loving of all dogs is the Newfoundland.

[189]

§ 479

That a man always dislikes his mother-in-law, and goes half-crazy every time she visits him.

§ 480

That St. Louis in summer is the hottest place in the world.

§ 481

That all the men in the moving picture business were formerly cloak and suit merchants, and that they are now all millionaires.

§ 482

That the accumulation of money makes a man hard, and robs him of all his finer qualities.

§ 483

That, in an elevator, it is always a man who usurps the looking-glass.

§ 484

That it is very unlucky to wear an opal.

§ 485

That if a man's eyebrows meet, it is a sign that he has a very unpleasant nature.

§ 486

That a negro ball always ends up in a grand free-for-all fight, in which several coons are mortally slashed with razors.

§ 487

That if Houdini were locked up in Sing Sing, he would manage to make his get-away in less than half an hour's time.

§ 488

That Bob Ingersoll is in hell.

§ 489

That monkey-glands will restore a man of 85 to the vigor of 21, and cause him to elope with a Swedish servant-girl and become the father of twins.

§ 490

That the Pullman conductor always has a lower berth in reserve and can fix it for you if he is properly approached.

§ 491

That if an understudy makes a hit, the regular actor or actress immediately gets well and never misses another performance.

§ 492

That Aaron Burr possessed an irresistible charm for all the women with whom he came in contact, and that the virtue of even the most strait-laced was a very poor risk if left in a room alone with him as long as ten minutes.

§ 493

That whenever Stonewall Jackson prayed before a battle, it was a sure sign that the fighting was going to be very sanguinary and that lots of Yankees would be out of luck.

[192]

§ 494

That all schoolchildren are inordinately happy but don't know it.

§ 495

That a goat will wax fat on a diet of tin cans and back numbers of the *Saturday Evening Post*.

§ 496

That a little girl who is markedly pretty between the years of six and ten will probably lose all of her physical charms before she is grown; and that one who, at the same age, is hideously ugly will probably develop into a rare beauty.

§ 497

That no atheist has ever seriously contemplated the stars or the growth of a jimpson weed.

§ 498

That all English schoolboys call their fathers "pater" and write excellent Latin verse.

[193]

§ 499

That very ugly people are usually fascinating.

§ 500

That any English naval officer can easily drink a quart of whiskey in an evening and show no signs of intoxication.

§ 501

That the movie editors steal all of the good plots from the scenarios which amateurs have submitted.

§ 502

That it takes the united efforts of a large Persian family forty years to make one dining-room rug.

§ 503

That whenever grown people talk scandal in the presence of children, the little tots promptly rush off to the neighbours and repeat it.

§ 504

That only about one out of every hundred American citizens has any idea of the real issues of the campaign when he votes on election day.

§ 505

That the chief duty of a fireman, when not engaged in answering alarms, is to sit next to a warm fire in the hose-house and play checkers.

§ 506

That paper-hangers leave a room in a complete mess after they have finished their work.

§ 507

That an illegitimate child is always more or less gifted with artistic promptings, and usually turns out to be a poet or a violinist.

§ 508

That a circus is never as good as its posters lead one to believe.

[195]

§ 509

That candy ruins the teeth.

§ 510

That buttermilk is excellent for the complexion.

§ 511

That one can infallibly tell a cigar is a good one if the ashes remain on the end and don't fall off.

§ 512

That all press-agents are liars.

§ 513

That jewellers, in cleaning or repairing costly baubles, invariably remove the original stones and insert others made of paste.

§ 514

That all moving pictures of English country life are staged in Fort Lee, New Jersey.

[196]

§ 515

That if one steps on a rusty tack one will inevitably get lock-jaw.

§ 516

That it helps a young man in business if he grows a moustache.

§ 517

That barbers are inordinately loquacious.

§ 518

That having a baby interferes with an actress' career.

§ 519

That when one takes one's best girl buggy riding the horse never respects the situation.

§ 520

That when one buys a promising looking package at a sale of unclaimed freight, it always con-

[197]

tains a set of burglar tools or the collected works of F. Marion Crawford.

§ 521

That the French steamship lines serve excellent wine gratis.

§ 522

That a policeman is never around when he is wanted.

§ 523

That the negro is absolutely unreliable, and that it is impossible to count upon him doing what he promises to do.

§ 524

That Theda Bara was born in Arabia.

§ 525

That the invariable dessert in a third-rate boarding house is stewed prunes.

[198]

§ 526

That Clara Morris was so good in "Camille" because she used to go around to the hospitals and study the way women suffering from tuberculosis died.

§ 527

That one can buy practically everything in Kokomo that is on sale in the Rue de la Paix.

§ 528

That home-cooking is far more appetizing than that in the best restaurant.

§ 529

That all graduates of Harvard wear horn-rimmed spectacles and speak with a marked English accent.

§ 530

That before the Volstead act nobody ever attempted a round of golf without drinking ten cocktails, and that since national prohibition the aver-

[199]

age player has reduced his record for the course by at least five strokes.

§ 531

That a young man who fails in business invariably dances the tango with great skill.

§ 532

That no traveller ever remembers anything of Rome except the fact that he paid $7 a day for his room and had to walk down the hallway to get a bath.

§ 533

That neither of the parties to a stage kiss derives any enjoyment from it.

§ 534

That no college professor understands baseball, but that every college professor sneaks off at periodic intervals to enjoy a good hot burlesque show.

§ 535

That all insane people insist that they are sane.

[200]

§ 536

That all patent-medicines are hooch in disguise.

§ 537

That seagulls fly around and around, never alighting until they drop dead from exhaustion.

§ 538

That motion-picture directors always throw away the working 'script after the first scene, and make up the action as the play progresses.

§ 539

That country garage-keepers sprinkle the nearby roads with crushed glass.

§ 540

That revenue officials imbibe at least three-fourths of the booze that they confiscate.

§ 541

That no matter how badly she wants to be kissed,
[201]

a girl will demur for a time just to make things interesting.

§ 542

That clergymen slip on store collars with ties attached whenever they leave their sacred duties, and raise hell in general.

§ 543

That any dish which has a French name is covered with a sauce that looks like glue.

§ 544

That a young man who inherits $100,000 invariably squanders his fortune before he is thirty-five.

§ 545

That all the most successful sirens are blondes.

§ 546

That rich women invariably dress in dowdy
[202]

fashion and are mistaken for the servants of their French maids.

§ 547

That women who are able to afford servants wear kimonos during the greater part of the day and read best sellers.

§ 548

That deacons drive hard bargains.

§ 549

That farm hands begin each day by eating three dozen pancakes.

§ 550

That New Yorkers are the most provincial people in the world.

§ 551

That men who commute finally grow not to mind it.

§ 552

That suburbanites always leave a play before it

[203]

is over so that they can catch the last train home.

§ 553

That steamer acquaintances never become real friends.

§ 554

That trapeze performers often fall on purpose, in order to convince the audience of the difficulties of their profession.

§ 555

That all the poetry in magazines is bad, and is accepted merely to fill up blank spaces at the bottom of a page.

§ 556

That the woman writer on an evening newspaper who gives advice to the lovelorn is invariably a man with a flowing beard.

§ 557

That all moving picture scenarios fetch fabulous prices.

[204]

§ 558

That tailors do not mind how long you keep them waiting for their money.

§ 559

That, if a woman constantly bleaches her hair, she is in danger of going insane.

§ 560

That garrulous people never have anything worth saying.

§ 561

That most people would steal a million dollars if they were sure they'd never be caught.

§ 562

That Maude Adams and David Warfield almost go mad because they are forced to play one part so long.

§ 563

That only millionaires go to Newport.

[205]

§ 564

That no one ever gets a full night's sleep in a sleeping-car.

§ 565

That lots of fashionable people eat at Childs' restaurants simply because they like good griddle cakes and coffee.

§ 566

That it is possible to overcome seasickness by sucking the juice of a lemon.

§ 567

That all men who wear beards do so in order to conceal weak chins.

§ 568

That the futurist painters are all insane.

§ 569

That, if you lend money, you lose the friendship of the recipient of your kindness.

[206]

§ 570

That any play by a Russian author is sordid and certain to give one the blues.

§ 571

That newspaper reporters can write without difficulty, no matter how much noise and confusion is around them.

§ 572

That the beer you brew at home is just as good as that made in Munich.

§ 573

That as soon as the American Army landed in France half of the men in each French company were allowed to go home to help their wives swindle the Americans.

§ 574

That a man who has five children stands more chance of being elected President than a man who has none.

[207]

§ 575

That all artists are impractical.

§ 576

That opportunity comes at least once to every man.

§ 577

That people who live in New York never have a moment to themselves.

§ 578

That the reason bachelors hate to visit happily married couples is that it makes them miserable with envy.

§ 579

That widows are far more dangerous than débutantes.

§ 580

That women who worry about losing their beauty age much faster than those who don't.

[208]

§ 581

That whenever a group of men get together they immediately begin discussing booze and women.

§582

That if a woman gives a man a letter to mail, it will remain in his pocket for a week.

§ 583

That all long-haired men are effeminate, and all short-haired women are masculine.

§ 584

That prohibition, whatever its faults, is a good thing for the workingman.

§ 585

That being in love with a beautiful woman is a great inspiration to an artist.

§ 586

That it is always necessary to tie ribbons on the
[209]

wrists of twins to keep Beulah from being confused with Otto.

§ 587

That there is something the matter with a man who can tell a Louis XV clock from a salt cellar by Benvenuto Cellini.

§ 588

That Abraham Lincoln was the originator of the smoking car story.

§ 589

That all young widows prolong the period of mourning if they think black becoming.

§ 590

That all negroes have perfect white teeth.

§ 591

That the editorial staff of *The Liberator* is composed entirely of anarchists, who are very violent characters.

§ 592

That if a sailor dies on board a ship, a shark becomes promptly cognizant of the fact and proceeds to follow the ship all the way across the ocean.

§ 593

That the *Boston Transcript* is written entirely by college professors, and that its English is so good that common people can't understand it.

§ 594

That no woman can throw straight, and that if she aims a brick at the mantelpiece it will hit the bookcase behind her.

§ 595

That all of Woodrow Wilson's shortcomings were due to his having been a college professor.

§ 596

That dramatic critics get many invitations from beautiful actresses to dine with them alone in their

[211]

boudoirs, and that the beautiful actresses there make love to them in order to get good notices.

§ 597

That a sharp man may for ten cents often pick up in a second-hand book-store a book that is worth a hundred dollars.

§ 598

That while the days in California are very warm, the evenings are always so cool that one has to wear an overcoat.

§ 599

That Ruth Law was in reality a German boy shrewdly disguised.

§ 600

That the mutual confidences of boarding-school girls are very racy.

§ 601

That the late Grover Cleveland was a great booze-fighter, and used to carry on like a drunken sailor at the White House.

§ 602

That if one sleeps with the moonlight shining full in one's face, one will go insane.

§ 603

That if one's nose itches, it is a sign that some-one is coming to visit.

§ 604

That both Abraham Lincoln and Jefferson Davis were the illegitimate sons of Henry Clay.

§ 605

That a negro who wears gold-rimmed spectacles never actually needs them, but affects them because they make him look intelligent.

§ 606

That the liquid contained in the centre of many golf balls will cause instant total blindness.

§ 607

That when one asks a bell-boy in a hotel in Buda-Pest to get one's suit pressed, he reappears in a few minutes with a large blonde.

§ 608

That the description of the Battle of the Marne in "The Four Horsemen of the Apocalypse" is a wonderful piece of writing.

§ 609

That all the officers of the United States Navy, before the day of Josephus Daniels, were terrific boozers, and that it was a common thing for them to run a battleship ashore, at a cost to the taxpayers of $9,000,000.

§ 610

That if one spills salt, one should throw a pinch over one's left shoulder to ward off ill luck.

§ 611

That when some one walks between a couple,

[214]

each of them should say "bread and butter" to ward off a quarrel.

§ 612

That when one sees a red-headed woman, one is sure to see a white horse within a block.

§ 613

That it is bad luck to see the new moon over one's left shoulder.

§ 614

That carrying a nutmeg in one's pocket will prevent rheumatism.

§ 615

That a piece of bread and butter, if dropped, will always fall butter side down.

§ 616

That before the war whenever the American ambassador in Berlin attended a diplomatic function he would be insulted by German high officials who would crack jokes about the United States.

§ 617

That rapping on wood will ward off calamity.

§ 618

That if one's corns hurt, it is a sign that it is going to rain.

§ 619

That if one dreams of falling and dreams that one lands, one will never awaken and will be dead.

§ 620

That if one saves the pennies, the dollars will save themselves.

§ 621

That to have a black cat cross one's path means bad luck.

§ 622

That when a man consults his watch he always forgets what time it is the instant after he has replaced it in his pocket.

[216]

§ 623

That cockroaches born in the morning are great-grandfathers before evening.

§ 624

That thunder sours fresh milk.

§ 625

That when one of the ultra-fashionable set gives a house-party the guests do nothing but lounge around, drink cocktails, and engage in a great deal of very witty repartee.

§ 626

That there are a vast number of desperate underworld characters who will engage to murder anybody for a sum not exceeding one dollar and fifty cents.

§ 627

That French ladies' maids during their idle moments amuse themselves by peeping through the key-holes of bedroom doors.

[217]

§ 628

That women search their husbands' pants pockets at night and appropriate all the loose change.

§ 629

That to drop a dish-rag signifies that company is coming.

§ 630

That one can greatly increase one's chest expansion by standing in front of an open window every morning and taking twenty-five deep breaths.

§ 631

That at every fashionable wedding there are present no less than a dozen detectives who are engaged to watch the valuable gifts, and that nobody can ever distinguish the detectives from the guests.

§ 632

That people who live far away from New York know far more about the town than the natives do.

[218]

§ 633

That if one is having bad luck in a card game a great change of fortune is effected by walking around one's chair.

§ 634

That all policemen have unduly large feet.

§ 635

That people suffering from tuberculosis are always very optimistic and feel sure that there is nothing the matter with them.

§ 636

That old ladies enjoy attending a funeral and that they always obtain front-row seats.

§ 637

That when a man on the streets gazes at a woman wearing abbreviated skirts his evil nature is awakened, but that if he were to see the same woman in a bathing suit the sight of her would leave him cold.

§ 638

That when one swallows a needle it travels through the body for years and years and ultimately emerges somewhere in the region of the little toe.

§ 639

That if a young swain can watch his girl eat corn on the cob and still have any love for her, his affection is genuine.

§ 640

That the cooks who prepare griddle cakes in the front windows of Childs' restaurants are all expert jugglers.

§ 641

That a man who lives to be a hundred years old always takes a glass of whiskey a day and uses tobacco freely.

§ 642

That if a demi-rep really falls in love with a man she is always faithful to him to the bitter end.

[220]

§ 643

That if China could organize an army in proportion to its population it could conquer the world in about three weeks.

§ 644

That when an old maid retires at night she always looks under the bed for a burglar, and that if she were to discover one she would immediately lock the door and throw the key out of the window.

§ 645

That when a Frenchman gets in a free-for-all fight he always strikes out with his feet instead of his fists.

§ 646

That it is extremely hazardous to drink well-water in the dark since one is likely to swallow a pollywog.

§ 647

That the director of an orchestra makes a great

many gestures merely to show off and that the music would be almost as good if there were no leader at all.

§ 648

That when a small boy is having his photograph taken he will remain very quiet if one tells him that a little bird is about to emerge from the camera.

§ 649

That people of Oriental blood always have very wily natures and that they glide about without making a sound.

§ 650

That when a military spy is caught he always has in his possession a small but extremely valuable piece of paper which he immediately proceeds to chew up and swallow.

§ 651

That middle-aged widows are very fond of college boys.

§ 652

That the headwaiter in every fashionable restaurant owns a block of apartments and a Rolls-Royce.

§ 653

That the first thing the Bolsheviks did in Russia was to nationalize the women, and that all of the most toothsome cuties were reserved for Trotsky and Lenin.

§ 654

That no matter how angry a woman may be at her husband he can always appease her wrath by giving her enough money to buy a new hat.

§ 655

That during the late war a great many society girls who acted as nurses cut up high jinks with the young soldiers.

§ 656

That when people who are unaccustomed to

[223]

money inherit a fortune their existence is likely
to become very miserable.

§ 657

That before long all the money in the country
will be in the hands of the Jews.

§ 658

That if the man in the end seat of a trolley car
yawns, every one else in the car will soon also be
yawning.

§ 659

That a person's sensations while drowning are
rather agreeable and that on the whole it is a very
pleasant death.

§ 660

That cows have very sad eyes.

§ 661

That raspberries taste better when eaten off the
bush.

§ 662

That acrobats could not do their stunts if they had not had their bones scientifically broken a few moments after they were born.

§ 663

That when two women enter a street car they always have a loud argument as to which one will stand the fare, but that as a matter of fact they are both bluffing and neither one wants to pay.

§ 664

That Chinese labourers work sixteen hours a day and are paid a weekly stipend of approximately eleven cents.

§ 665

That football is a very fine thing and greatly improves the moral character of college boys and that they never neglect an opportunity in the heat of a game to surreptitiously kick an opponent in the back of the head.

[225]

§ 666

That the men who pass the collection plates in Fifth Avenue churches always have a lot of loose change in their pockets on Monday morning.

§ 667

That the nurses in maternity hospitals are often careless and that the babies frequently get mixed up.

§ 668

That a youth who goes to Harvard, though he may learn nothing, is given a high polish.

§ 669

That many women who live in fashionable apartment houses have liaisons with the elevator boys.

§ 670

That the liquor problem is entirely due to corner saloons and that if there had never been such places nobody would have ever got drunk.

[226]

§ 671

That most women begin a street flirtation by dropping their handerchiefs.

§ 672

That a German never spends less than one hour consuming a single glass of beer.

§ 673

That women of the half world always carry all their money in their stockings.

§ 674

That American men have more respect for women than the men of any other country.

§ 675

That a flea is a very intelligent insect.

§ 676

That all the chorus girls in the Hippodrome are over forty years of age and have false teeth.

[227]

§ 677

That in a photoplay a motion picture actress brings tears to her eyes by concealing an onion in her handkerchief.

§ 678

That it is very dangerous to sleep in a folding bed since it is liable to close up in the middle of the night and smother one to death.

§ 679

That the Indians in wild west shows are in reality not Indians at all but painted Chinamen.

§ 680

That a man who is sitting in front of one will turn around if one concentrates one's attention on the back of his head.

§ 681

That a dexterous pickpocket can actually extract a roll of bills from the inside of one's undershirt without one being the wiser.

[228]

§ 682

That a young man who holds a position of trust in the financial world is constantly shadowed by detectives and that if he were to dine with a chorus girl he would immediately lose his job.

§ 683

That women who loll about the beaches in stunning bathing costumes never go near the water.

§ 684

That whenever a bank fails the president is always a venerable grey-haired man who either commits suicide or goes to jail.

§ 685

That French actresses never hesitate to appear on the stage perfectly nude.

§ 686

That people who sit in the gallery at a play are more discriminating than those in the orchestra.

[229]

§ 687

That when a man falls from a great height he always loses consciousness before he hits the ground.

§ 688

That most men, when dressed in evening clothes, can hardly be distinguished from waiters.

§ 689

That convicts like their existence in the new reformed prisons so much that they often refuse to leave when their terms have expired.

§ 690

That a Mason who reveals the secrets of the order will mysteriously disappear and never be heard of again.

§ 691

That Daniel Webster delivered his greatest orations when he was so drunk that he had to hold on to a table to stand up.

§ 692

That when Italians make wine they always press the grapes with their bare feet.

§ 693

That all star intercollegiate sprinters die of enlargement of the heart.

§ 694

That the most beneficial sleep is that which comes before midnight.

§ 695

That people with red hair are more directly descended from monkeys than the rest of mankind.

§ 696

That professors are absent-minded, that they often come to their classes minus collar or tie, and that they sometimes walk into other people's homes by mistake while engrossed in deep thought.

§ 697

That a pitcher on a baseball team is not expected to hit.

§ 698

That when they drop anything on the floor in a canning factory they put it into the can without washing it, no matter how dirty the floor is.

§ 699

That a Chinaman may kill his wife for less than nothing, and need never even go into court to explain his conduct.

§ 700

That a negro will not work so long as he has a nickel in his pocket.

§ 701

That when a man tells you that he was born in Virginia it is a sign that he will try to sell you a gold brick or some oil stock.

[232]

§ 702

That all Irishmen are very witty, and when engaged in an argument invariably crush their opponents with a final excruciatingly funny remark.

§ 703 ·

That all professors at German universities spend their evenings in beer-gardens, and that each one slowly sips from twenty-five to forty steins of lager before retiring.

§ 704

That all French poets stay hooched up on absinthe and produce their most sublime works when in a semi-demented condition.

§ 705

That the capacity of any negro boy for watermelon is unlimited.

§ 706

That laundry wagon drivers are mostly college graduates.

§ 707

That if an Irishman were shipwrecked on a cannibal island he would be married to the chief's daughter and running the joint inside of a week.

§ 708

That all Methodist deacons, when they visit a city, get hilariously drunk and spend their time at leg shows and disreputable resorts.

§ 709

That people who are born rich are never vain, and that people who are born poor and later become rich are always vain.

§ 710

That when a hard boiled guy gets married he usually becomes so respectable that it hurts.

§ 711

That Edgar Allan Poe wrote all his stuff while sobering up after sprees.

[234]

§ 712

That England always persuades some other country to do her fighting for her, and that, when both her ally and her enemy are exhausted, she comes in strong at the finish and reaps all the benefits from the war.

§ 713

That when an Indian falls in love with a white woman and she refuses to marry him he never loses his self-possession, but goes back to his own people and lies around in the sun wrapped in a blanket.

§ 714

That summer romances are forgotten with the first frost.

§ 715

That in the days of chivalry all the Knights Errant were gallant to all the women they met, said their prayers every night before retiring, drank a little, but did not swear.

[235]

§ 716

That if you are familiar with a negro once, he will shove you off the sidewalk into the gutter the next time he meets you.

§ 717

That only a small percentage of Americans know more than a few lines of "The Star-Spangled Banner," and that they are so unfamiliar with the tune that they are always getting to their feet when the band plays "How Dry I am."

§ 718

That the French and English were eager to give up and make peace on the Kaiser's terms when the United States horned in and forced them to go on.

§ 719

That if one tries on a suit of clothes in a Jewish clothing store one is always told that it is a perfect fit, no matter if it hangs like a coat upon a rack or clings like the paper to the wall.

[236]

§ 720

That old negro mammies, now fast becoming extinct, always refer to their "white folks" as "honey chile."

§ 721

That a piece of asafœtida worn about the neck will ward off various diseases.

§ 722

That born and bred Virginians and South Carolinians are very proud of their origin and are given to excessive braggadocio.

§ 723

That in spite of the fact that all negroes make a great holiday of July the Fourth only about five per cent. of them know why they are celebrating.

§ 724

That when you've made up your mind to have a tooth extracted it always stops aching just as you place your hand on the dentist's doorknob.

[237]

§ 725

That persons with exceedingly high foreheads are always possessed of remarkable intelligence.

§ 726

That it is almost impossible to find a person living in New York who was born there.

§ 727

That drinking vinegar or the juice of a lemon will reduce one's weight.

§ 728

That all negroes love funerals and circuses, and turn out in great numbers to attend them both, arrayed in their best clothes.

§ 729

That a fortune-teller invariably says that you are going on a long journey, will cross water, and had better beware of a certain dark person who is trying to make trouble.

[238]

§ 730

That nowhere is such hospitality found as south of the Mason and Dixon line.

§ 731

That the quivering cry of a screech owl heard just outside a house is a sign that some one in the house will shortly die.

§ 732

That seaside building lots are under the water a greater part of the time.

§ 733

That it is impossible to learn a foreign language at college.

§ 734

That when people read a patent medicine pamphlet they immediately become convinced that they are suffering from all the diseases described therein.

[239]

§ 735

That a husband is tickled to death when his wife goes away to the country.

§ 736

That a negro eats nothing but pork chops and chicken, and that he always has a razor handy.

§ 737

That popular song writers always steal their melodies from well known operas.

§ 738

That a clever Central Office detective knows the face of every crook in town.

§ 739

That only a millionaire can afford to play polo.

§ 740

That when one is taking a bath it is very difficult to keep the soap under control.

§ 741

That a Jew always outwits a Christian in a business deal.

§ 742

That one always gets tired of a blonde quicker than a brunette.

§ 743

That the chief purpose of music in hotel dining-rooms is to drown the noise of people eating soup.

§ 744

That people go abroad and visit historic places for the sole purpose of being able to brag about it.

§ 745

That a married man never enjoys kissing his wife.

§ 746

That a man's wife is never as good a cook as his mother.

[241]

§ 747

That the women of backwoods communities have learned how to dress as a result of watching motion pictures.

§ 748

That when a girl who has been raised in poor circumstances marries, she demands a lot of expensive jewelry, four automobiles, three country houses, and a large staff of servants; but that when a girl who is accustomed to every luxury marries, she is perfectly willing to sew, cook, wash, take care of the baby, and darn her husband's socks.

§ 749

That people with a strong physique are more likely to succumb to an illness than those who look delicate.

§ 750

That as a result of prohibition all wealthy Americans who like to tipple will go abroad and spend the rest of their lives there.

[242]

§ 751

That all of the Americans taken prisoner by the Bolsheviki were innocent.

§ 752

That in Japan all the positions of trust in the banks are held by Chinamen.

§ 753

That in English families of title, the younger sons always cut up high jinks, and have to be sent out of the country because of gambling debts or escapades with women.

§ 754

That you can judge a man by what newspaper he reads.

§ 755

That a few minutes before an atheist dies he usually changes his mind and becomes deeply religious, and that if he fails to do so he dies in great agony.

[243]

§ 756

That at every girls' boarding school there are several female rakes who do nothing but smoke cigarettes, tell risqué stories, and put the other girls hep to a lot of things they should not know.

§ 757

That some day Canada will become a part of the United States.

§ 758

That artists' models, while posing, frequently faint from exhaustion.

§ 759

That, in the old days, whenever a millionaire gave a midnight supper party a semi-clad chorus girl would dance on the table, and the guests would drink champagne out of her slipper.

§ 760

That people in the theatrical profession never take marriage seriously.

§ 761

That indigent men always pawn their winter overcoats when the warm weather begins.

§ 762

That the crowned heads of Continental Europe have vast quantities of illegitimate children.

§ 763

That when a man is suffering from misfortune he is always greatly cheered up by meeting a friend who is also in woe.

§ 764

That up until twenty years ago all physicians affected beards, but that they no longer do so because it is considered unsanitary.

§ 765

That at the time of the American Revolution everybody in England was in favour of giving the colonies their liberty and that the war only took place because of the obstinacy of the king, who was very pro-German.

§ 766

That finger bowls are really of no value and are merely used as a matter of form.

§ 767

That when a bride and groom arrive at an hotel resort they never are able to disguise the fact that they have just been married.

§ 768

That if an undertaker were to discover that a supposedly dead person was still alive, he would immediately inject poison into the body in order not to lose the job.

§ 769

That a man who loudly declares that he intends always to remain a bachelor always marries the first pretty girl he meets.

[246]

§ 770

That there is no future for a man who works in a bank.

§ 771

That when a subway conductor calls out the names of the stations nobody can understand him.

§ 772

That no matter how courageous a man may be he is always afraid to visit a dentist.

§ 773

That parents suffer great mental anguish when they whip their children.

§ 774

That people who offer one a firm handclasp are very upright and honest.

§ 775

That a high-minded man and woman never kiss each other until the man proposes marriage.

[247]

§ 776

That a man who follows horse-racing goes broke sooner or later.

§ 777

That a minister's son usually grows up to be a drunkard or a thief.

§ 778

That most people who own automobiles cannot afford them.

§ 779

That when a man of little breeding attends a banquet he never knows what spoon or fork to use.

§ 780

That no matter how happy a bride may be she always weeps on her wedding day.

§ 781

That in London all clerks go to work at ten A. M., quit at 3 P. M., and wear silk hats.

[248]

§ 782

That when one drops a penny in a chewing gum slot machine, the chances are that nothing will come out.

§ 783

That the chief pastime of young medical students is hurling human arms and legs at each other in the dissecting room.

§ 784

That you can get the best seat in the Grand Opera House at Milan for twenty cents.

§ 785

That if Theodore Roosevelt had been president when the War began he would have ended it within three weeks.

§ 786

That a man who falls in love with a married woman is rotten to the core and is capable of any crime from murder to petty larceny.

§ 787

That a beautiful woman never has any brains.

§ 788

That if a waiter in a restaurant has a grudge against one he will surreptitiously spit into one's food.

§ 789

That the Haitians still practise cannibalism.

§ 790

That young girls only smoke cigarettes because they think it looks smart.

§ 791

That the only people who really appreciate opera are Italian barbers.

§ 792

That if one is in a great hurry to get some place, one is always greatly delayed en route.

[250]

§ 793

That a great many society women use very pro-
fane language.

§ 794

That a tremendous amount of sickness is caused
by drinking ice water.

§ 795

That a person who has little to say is very wise
and a profound thinker.

§ 796

That people who live in Brooklyn have a great
many babies.

§ 797

That to pay a bill in cash causes one a great
deal more anguish than to pay it with a cheque.

§ 798

That people who purloin spoons from hotel din-

ing-rooms and keep them as souvenirs are honest in
every other way.

§ 799

That when two young girls who room together
return from a party they always lie awake all
night and talk about it.

§ 800

That when a woman has a row with her husband she always cries and threatens to return to
her mother.

§ 801

That at a wedding nobody ever pays any attention to the bridegroom.

§ 802

That every small village has a haunted house.

§ 803

That a human being's heart stops beating one
instant in the middle of the night.

[252]

§ 804

That up to fifteen years' ago people always went to Niagara Falls for their honeymoon.

§ 805

That professional card sharps always dress immaculately and have very ingratiating manners.

§ 806

That in a crowded car a man never offers his seat to a woman unless she is very beautiful.

§ 807

That a young man must engage in a certain amount of deviltry before he settles down.

§ 808

That people who go to church a great deal are either fanatics or hypocrites.

§ 809

That a bride always looks very pretty.

[253]

§ 810

That people who receive complimentary seats for the theatre always roast the play.

§ 811

That battleships are of no further fighting value, and that they are only constructed for the convenience of admirals who use them as they would private yachts.

§ 812

That the Germans never invent anything themselves, but that they appropriate the most ingenious inventions of other people.

§ 813

That it is easier to teach a mongrel dog tricks than a thoroughbred.

§ 814

That whether a New Englander is in Siberia, Hindustan, Alaska or Flatbush, he always returns home for Thanksgiving.

§ 815

That an after-dinner speech is always very tire-some.

§ 816

That most women's diseases are the result of modern fashions in dress.

§ 817

That everybody who signed the Declaration of Independence was a great man.

§ 818

That the late war was decided upon years ago by Bismarck, who, in formulating his plans, freely consulted Nietzsche.

§ 819

That when Lee surrendered to Grant there was a very touching scene; that Lee offered Grant his sword, which Grant declined and that Grant then offered Lee a cigar and a swig out of a pint of whiskey, which Lee accepted.

§ 820

That hasty marriages are bound to end disastrously.

§ 821

That the men who own the hat-checking privileges in New York restaurants are all millionaires.

§ 822

That there is a strange and mysterious difference between people who live in Manhattan and people who live in Brooklyn.

§ 823

That it makes no difference when one drops tobacco ashes on the carpet, because the ashes help to preserve it.

§ 824

That when one of the houris in a Turkish seraglio misbehaves, she is immediately sewn up in a sack and dropped through a trap-door into a subterranean river.

[256]

§ 825

That if one goes out wearing new clothes it is sure to rain.

§ 826

That a tremendous amount of kidney trouble is due to motorcycles and jitney automobiles.

§ 827

That when a woman driving an automobile gets into a tight place she promptly loses her head and causes an accident.

§ 828

That if one were to read the dictionary ten minutes each day one would become very learned.

§ 829

That the Rev. Dr. Billy Sunday has made $1,000,000 out of his gospel business.

§ 830

That when a Spaniard is in love he hangs

[257]

around all night beneath the window of his inamo-
rata and serenades her with a guitar.

§ 831

That London women have beautiful complexions, which they owe entirely to the fogs.

§ 832

That young people become especially amorous
in the springtime.

§ 833

That Isaac Newton discovered the law of gravity
because, as a boy, an apple fell off a tree and
fetched him a bang on the coco.

§ 834

That Edgar Allan Poe was always drunk except
when he took morphine.

§ 835

That in every family the father is partial to
the girl and the mother to the son.

[258]

§ 836

That if a man tries to flirt with a woman at a little distance and she looks with curiosity at his feet, he will be so overcome by embarrassment that he will retreat.

§ 837

That the current craze for spiritualism is the result of propaganda financed by the men who manufacture ouija boards.

§ 838

That the monocle worn by an Englishman is made of cheap window glass, and that whenever he wants to see anything he has to drop it out of his eye.

§ 839

That the late J. Pierpont Morgan was the easiest mark the fake antique dealers of Europe had discovered in 250 years, and that a syndicate of Italians actually built five factories in Italy for the sole purpose of manufacturing fake Rembrandts to sell to him.

§ 840

That when peroxide of hydrogen is applied to an open wound, the ensuing bubbling shows that the wound is being efficaciously disinfected.

§ 841

That since the war all the French atheists have become devout Catholics.

§ 842

That England entered the war in order to discharge an obligation of honour to Belgium.

§ 843

That Southerners are chivalrous.

§ 844

That all college girls wear glasses and are very ugly.

§ 845

That all men who want to work very little and get a lot of money for it are Bolsheviki.

§ 846

That the life of a young man who marries an old woman for her money is always a very miserable and unhappy one.

§ 847

That prize-fighters are very good to their mothers, and that they are drunk all the time they are not training for a match.

§ 848

That in all the battles of the late war, both on the eastern front and on the western front, the German hordes enormously outnumbered the small and gallant bands of Russians, Frenchmen, Italians, Rumanians, Portuguese, Sikhs, Cambodians, Irishmen, Scotchmen, Welchmen, Canadians, Australians, New Zealanders, Somalis, Greeks, Singalese and Americans who opposed them.

§ 849

That water drunk from the washstand faucet is not as pure as water drunk from the kitchen faucet.

§ 850

That if a child eats snow he will get diphtheria.

§ 851

That all professional strong men are muscle-bound.

§ 852

That men who are good to animals are often wife-beaters.

§ 853

That a baby knows instinctively whether a man is good or bad.

§ 854

That there are a lot of things which are very good in theory but wont work in practice.

§ 855

That if all the money in the world were to be divided, within a year the same men would have it again.

§ 856

That although 200 per cent. of Washington's army deserted at one time or another, the patriotism and valour of the Continentals should set us a great example.

§ 857

That the late Theodore Roosevelt got a dollar a word for all his magazine writings.

§ 858

That the French make great soldiers; that the English Tommy is a great soldier; that the Canadians make great soldiers; that the Australians, Germans, Belgians and Americans make great soldiers; that the Cossacks are great soldiers; that the Japs make great little soldiers, etc., etc.

§ 859

That the French, Dutch, Belgians, Jews, Scotch and Germans are very thrifty peoples; that the Italians save every cent they make; that the New England Yankee is very economical; that the Chi-

nese and Japanese live on rice and are extraordinarily thrifty; that, in fact, no one is improvident
and extravagant except Americans in New York
and Paris, and all Irishmen.

§ 860

That if all the coal in the world should suddenly
give out, science would quickly devise something
in its stead.

§ 861

That it always takes a woman at least an hour
and a half to dress, whereas a man finishes the
job in three minutes.

§ 862

That Henry Ford is against the Jews because he
tried to borrow $50,000,000 from them and they
demanded 10 per cent. a month.

§ 863

That all the girls in Richmond, Va., are great
beauties, but that they will not look at a Yankee.

§ 864

That Baltimore is the place to eat oysters, and that the folks down there are all epicures and live on the fat of the land.

§ 865

That the Pennsylvania Dutch are all very rich, but that they can't speak English and never take a bath.

§ 866

That the late war was caused by the Kaiser single-handed, and that his plan was to seize all of Europe, reduce the inhabitants to slavery, and then conquer the United States.

§ 867

That every dollar-a-year man during the war swindled the government out of at least $1,000,000.

§ 868

That President Harding was nominated at

Chicago as a result of a clever trick arranged by Col. George W. Harvey, and that Harvey was made Ambassador to England as a reward.

§ 869

That a war with England would probably be a good thing, inasmuch as the English would be afraid to cross the ocean, and so the United States would have a chance to grab both Canada and Mexico.

(The End)